Whatever Works

A Toolkit for Self-Optimization

🌐 WhateverWorks.me

RON GROSS

Ballast Books, LLC
www.ballastbooks.com

Copyright © 2025 by Ron Gross

ISBN: 978-1-964934-56-3

Printed in the United States of America

Published by Ballast Books

To toolmakers and tool users

TABLE OF CONTENTS

INTRODUCTION

Few, if any, of us get through the day feeling as though there is nothing that could have been improved. The desire to make things better is an essential element of being human, and most of us actively wish that aspects of our lives were better in some way. Sometimes it's the little things that bother us, like a smartphone distracting us with beeps or dings while we're trying to have a face-to-face conversation. At other times, we wrestle with larger problems, such as an inability to resolve a conflict with our partner. In between, we may wish we were in better shape, want our memory to be sharper, desire more refreshing sleep, or strive for a sense of connection with something greater than ourselves. There are all sorts of ways we could improve our lives . . . if only we had the tools to do so.

Most of us, however, are not used to thinking about self-improvement in these terms. We may resist the idea that we need to use a *tool* to achieve the results we seek. Perhaps applying the concept of tools to sensitive parts of our lives, such as our psyches, seems mechanical and inhuman, or we resist the connotation that there is something wrong with us that needs to be fixed. The tools in this book, however, are not necessarily meant to repair anything or anyone, or even imply that anyone is broken. They are simply processes, methods, and techniques that offer the possibility of better outcomes tomorrow than we can achieve today.

Life Is Complex

The sheer complexity of life can create chaotic situations and plenty of stress. None of us are perfect. We are all works in progress, evolving in our own ways and directions.

We are all working on numerous projects and activities, both in our work and our personal lives. Professional, romantic, and familial relationships require our time and attention, each of them coming with their own obligations and responsibilities. It's a lot to juggle and manage, and it's impossible to do everything perfectly all the time, which is why finding methods—or tools—to improve and grow in each of these areasis sometimes necessary to carve out order from the chaos and ease the stress.

Even when things are going well, most of us can still find ways to optimize some aspects of our lives. The software in our phones and computers is constantly being updated to improve its performance. In the same way, we can seek to update our behavior. And when we do, we may discover deeper levels of productivity and ease, whether at work or at play. We learn we can indeed have more satisfying relationships and better mental, emotional, and physical health.

Yet the plethora of available tools can feel as mind-boggling as life itself. If you regularly engage in self-improvement, you may already be familiar with the sense of being overwhelmed that can ensue from attempting to parse this complex field. Amazon lists more than ninety thousand books in the "self-improvement" category. Choosing the most effective tool can be so confusing that it feels like it's not worth the effort.

It doesn't have to be that way.

Grab Your Tools

For many years, I've been curating tools for my personal use. The ones compiled in this book represent those I've found most effective, and I hope that you will experiment by applying them to your life and optimizing whatever areas you feel can be improved. Beyond providing you with individual techniques and concepts that you find useful, this book's meta-goal is to teach tool-based thinking, encouraging you to discover and develop your own set of tools. You are also invited to contribute suggestions and new tools back to the community online at whateverworks.me.

In some chapters, I've designated one tool as a Pillar because it has impacted me greatly and I use it on a day-to-day basis. These Pillar tools, marked with the symbol ▊, are more comprehensive than others, consisting of more detailed concepts and instructions for their use. They are:

▊ Getting Things Done

▊ Nonviolent Communication

▊ Meditation

▊ Jordan Peterson's Twelve Rules for Life

All the tools are grouped into six different chapters, except for one, which falls under the heading of "Meta Tool: Seek Continuous Improvement." It's listed this way because it forms the principle that underpins every other tool and thereby deserves to be considered uniquely. After the Meta tool, you'll find the rest separated into specific chapters. Categorizing the tools was a challenge in itself because several could have fit into more than one chapter. I've placed them where I think they make the most sense and fit in most seamlessly with other tools. Some tools are loosely related to others. In those instances, you'll find a note cross-referencing the location of the connected tool.

Each tool opens with a description of the **motivation** for utilizing it. This is important—otherwise, why bother? Below this, I've provided a short summary of the key **benefits** of learning and applying the tool, along with the accompanying **challenges**. Below these sections, you'll find the **application,** which discusses how to practice the tool and/or provides examples of it in practice. Finally, if there is **further reading** that can provide more information, it is listed at the end.

This book serves as a compendium. All told, there are almost a hundred tools here. For the simplest tools, the application section provides enough information to begin using the tool immediately. In some cases, however, whole books have been written about one tool alone, and space doesn't allow me to go into that level of depth. For these more detailed tools, the application section merely presents the method. In these cases, if you think a tool will work for you, you'll want to do a deep dive into the references provided so you can learn how to implement the tool fully.

Don't be scared by the number of tools. There's no need to aspire to apply every one. The purpose is to provide you with a selection from which you can pick and choose, discovering the tools that are most applicable to you (more on this later).

The chapters are as follows.

Productivity

Here you'll find tools that can help you better manage your time, attention, workflow, and projects. In this category, you'll find the Pillar tool Getting Things Done (GTD)—a comprehensive methodology for stress-free **Productivity**. There are also tools to help you keep distractions at bay and make better decisions. And because being productive often requires you to work effectively with others, there are tools to encourage cooperation and focus in a team setting. Finally, there are tools that help you rest from productivity. You cannot be productive all the time; you must allow your mind and body to rest and recharge.

Relationships

In the second chapter, you'll discover multiple tools aimed toward improving **Relationships** and communication and opening up channels of understanding. The Pillar tool Nonviolent Communication

(NVC) can help you form, maintain, and repair heart-to-heart authentic connections with others and yourself and also help you get more of everyone's needs met. The relationship tools apply to group settings, as well as to one-on-one situations in just about any type of relationship. There are also tools you can use to help you express your emotions and be more empathetic to yourself and to others.

Therapy

The third chapter contains tools that can assist you in getting the most out of **Therapy** in whatever form you receive it, whether your therapy takes place with a professional therapist or counselor or if you are walking a path of self-help. These tools also include methods for handling conflict and ways to connect with other people, providing a safe place where everyone can bring their whole selves to a conversation. Also included are methods for dealing with and managing difficult emotions. Jordan Peterson's Twelve Rules for Life are presented as the Pillar tool, as they offer some keys for leading a meaningful, authentic life (e.g., Rule 2: Treat yourself like you are someone you are responsible for helping).

Body

The second half of the book focuses on three areas: **Body**, **Mind**, and **Spirit**. In the **Body** chapter, you'll find tools centered on physical health and well-being. We all understand the importance of eating right and exercising, but neither strategy is always easy, pleasant, or even effective. The collection of tools in this chapter discusses various options for properly taking care of your body, including sports, exercise, diet, and supplements. You'll also read hacks intended to cut through resistance or lethargy and make it easier to stick to a particular nutritional plan or eating regimen. As usual, this book won't prescribe a specific course of action. It will instead present various options from which you can pick and choose, tailoring them to your specific needs.

Mind

Tools in the **Mind** chapter are dedicated to helping you remember things you've read or heard or people you've met. They're relevant to many aspects of the mind's functioning and should empower you to think critically, engage your creativity, and expand your openness to new ideas. You will find tools aimed at helping you improve your memory, address your fears, and relax your buzzing brain so that you can sleep more deeply. In combination, the tools in this chapter should improve your thinking and contribute to the development of a healthier brain.

Spirit

The final chapter groups together a selection of tools under the rubric of **Spirit**. These tools are geared toward the exploration of the philosophical and spiritual realms. They cover a broad range of terrain, from ideas for gaining perspective on suffering to strategies for developing a sense of connection to a power greater than ourselves. In particular, there are many tools exploring spiritual concepts, such as the illusion of separation, along with pitfalls, such as identifying too strongly with a desire for spiritual progress or a misplaced belief in one's enlightenment.

Why I Am Sharing These Tools

Although I began compiling these tools and techniques a few years ago, the drive to improve my life began at a young age when I realized the huge benefits that can be gained from optimizing repeated processes. Perhaps it is only natural, then, that when I became an adult, I worked as a software engineer—a discipline where I spent a lot of my time systematically creating processes and iteratively improving upon them in order to achieve better business results.

As I developed in my professional career, I held various managerial and entrepreneurial roles where I applied the concept of iterative improvement while dealing with rapidly changing environments, opportunities, and risks. In order to achieve better business results at work and handle the ever-increasing scope of work I was doing, productivity tools became increasingly important to me. I found, however, that they were also helpful in my personal life, where being organized and undistracted enabled me to work on my relationships.

In 2015, I began exploring concurrent polyamorous relationships. Although I'm no longer practicing polyamory, this period increased the requirements for clear and efficient communication and demanded an ability to connect emotionally with others in a sustainable manner. Because I found it imperative that I work hard on my relationships, I started looking for tools to help improve both my ability to be heard and my capacity to hear and understand others.

In 2013, I began to experience cycles of hypomania and depression due to a latent bipolar disorder only formally diagnosed in 2015. This led to a spiritual and emotional awakening. Knowing that my condition had a name was a huge relief, and learning that therapy could be conducive to improving my situation also brightened my general outlook on life. Over time, I found therapy to be so profoundly helpful that I began searching for tools to augment the benefits I was receiving. Since then, I have explored a variety of techniques in self-development from various teachers and sources, always seeking tools to complement my therapy sessions.

As I have come to understand my emotions more fully, I have also sought to invest in my physical health, putting more effort into an ongoing battle with cholesterol, triglycerides, and borderline high blood sugar. I've struggled at times with a memory that doesn't always retain the information I wish it would, making tools for developing the mind invaluable. The process of developing my body and mind has also contributed to a spiritual awakening, and many of the tools in this book have fueled my efforts to deepen my spiritual capacity and understand and integrate it more effectively into my daily life.

I've been involved with start-ups for several years and coached a few managers and start-up CEOs, so I quickly realized that I had a wide business network of people who were interested in the things I'd found helpful. Start-up CEOs, mid-level managers, and others asked me for business advice, and many also sought my help dealing with office politics, career development, and numerous other topics.

I discovered that I enjoyed helping others, and I received great feedback from those I helped. People told me that what I had to offer was truly useful. That was when I understood that I could encapsulate the tools and scale my teaching. I started by giving a presentation to teach what I'd learned, which at that point was mostly focused on productivity. The event was a success, and I proceeded to share this presentation with a few other start-ups. After the presentation, one organization even hung a poster of the Zuzunaga Diagram on their front door (see Tool 5.9: Find Your Purpose).

These presentations confirmed the value of what I had learned and led me to seek a medium to share the tools with even more people. I decided to create a book to make the tools more easily accessible for as many people as possible and to teach tool-based thinking.

How to Use This Book

This book is not a linear narrative. Therefore, it is not meant to be read from cover to cover. Instead, I suggest that you pick and choose subjects that you find especially interesting with the intention of finding a tool or two that could help you today in any area of your life. Apply these tools and assess the results. Then, try to incorporate them as long-term habits, or if you don't find them useful, drop them and experiment with others.

Occasionally, you might pass over a tool thinking it will not work for you, then return to it at a different point in your life and find that it is perfect for your new situation. Similarly, a tool may be dynamite today but gradually lose relevance as your life evolves. These tools are not presented dogmatically, as the answers to particular dilemmas in your life; they are offered in a spirit of flexibility, for you to explore and apply according to your needs. I recommend that you stay open to the tools in this book and be willing to give them a second chance if they don't work the first time. But please understand that no tool can replace your wisdom and intuition on when to use which tool and how to apply it.

One final note about the tools: They are always evolving. Feel free to tweak them to fit you and allow them to shift in ways that suit you. This is not only a book—it is also both a podcast and an open-source project, and the latest version of the tools is always available at whateverworks.me. You are encouraged to send in any suggestions, feedback, or new tools that you think can work.

Now, if you're ready, turn the page, and let's explore the fundamental Meta principle of continuous improvement that underlies this entire endeavor.

Meta Tool:
Seek Continuous Improvement

Dedicate some attention to thinking about how you can optimize whatever you're doing in the long run.

Motivation

Seldom are we ever completely happy and satisfied with our routines and habits. If we stop and think about what we are doing, we will find numerous opportunities to improve—we could be more productive, we could enjoy our workouts more, we could tweak our diets, we could have deeper conversations, and so on. The first step to optimization is opening ourselves up to thinking about the bigger picture and ways to improve it, rather than acting mindlessly.

Benefits

- Awareness allows you to take a step back and improve things.
- Even small changes, when compounded, have a significant impact.

Challenges

- Over-optimizing can make you lose focus on what you're doing.
- It can be hard to split your attention between present activities and ways you could act more effectively.

Application

There are two primary ways to adopt the concept of continuous improvement. The first is to dedicate some time specifically to optimization when you're otherwise unoccupied. The second is to think about how you can do things better *as you do them*, keeping a part of your brain focused on the task and another on how you can perform the task better next time.

When you're free to zoom out from the day-to-day tasks and challenges in your life and apply yourself to optimization, you can search for and identify the patterns of problems and annoyances, large and small, that occupy your life. This could be anything from always bumping against that desk at night on your way to the bathroom, to always forgetting to charge your headset, to deep issues in your marriage.

As you scan through whatever is troubling you, try to explore behaviors you could change, either practically or theoretically, to improve the situation. Break your behaviors down into concrete, actionable steps that can bring the desired improvement. It may take time and effort to execute these steps, and you may wish to consider whether the rewards are worth it. However, if the pattern of problems stretches over a sufficient time period or causes enough distress, you may decide that it's worth making a significant effort to improve the situation.

Once you begin this process, you can apply the changes, then review the effects as needed and course correct where appropriate.

A complementary way to apply this tool is in action, while you're doing an activity. The principle is the same; the difference is that you're looking for improvement in real time, as opposed to taking time out of your day in search of it. Whatever you are doing—sorting your laundry to prepare it for washing, working out at the gym, doing research for your work—try to place a portion of your attention on the next fifty, one hundred, or five hundred times you will perform the same action. Ask yourself whether there is a way you can optimize something *in the present* that will make it easier or better the next time you do it. Even if no solution comes to mind, spotting problems and noting them for later thought can often be helpful.

For example, let's say you pack a bag with both your laptop and a change of clothes so that when you're finished at the gym, you can shower and work at a café. If the bag is too small, you may find that you're squeezing sweaty gym clothes in with your laptop or having to bring an extra bag. (This is fine if you drive a car, but not so great if you're on a bike.) What's the solution? Perhaps, as you struggle to force everything into the bag, you realize that it's as simple as purchasing a larger bag, with separate compartments, so that you can keep your clothes and your laptop separate and carry them both with ease.

What's Next?

Tools—specifically the tools in this book—are a method of making things better. Without tools, humankind would never have evolved to the level of complexity that we have. At heart, every tool in this book is intended to offer you a suggestion you can use to improve your life.

You're invited to pick a chapter that you're interested in, scan the list of tools, and find one that piques your interest. Read it and see if you want to try it out. If not, keep going—there are plenty of other tools available to try.

CHAPTER ONE

PRODUCTIVITY

"Give me six hours to chop down a tree, and I will spend the first four sharpening my axe."

—Abe Lincoln (attributed)

P roductive people get things done. They work on projects, finish tasks, obtain results, and reach goals. In that sense, we are all productive to some degree. Many of us, however, aim to become more productive or manage our workloads and stress more effectively so that we have more time for loved ones and hobbies. We may wish to complete larger, more complex projects; experience fewer distractions or obstacles in our day-to-day lives; or simply experience a flow state—when we are absorbed in a challenging yet achievable task—more often. To this end, we must learn better time management skills, more organized thought processes, increased efficiency, and improved decision-making processes. The tools in this chapter are aimed at helping you improve in all these areas and more.

The purpose of these tools is not only to help you do more in less time but also to help you do more in the right direction, meaning that you actually move toward achieving meaningful life or business goals and doing things that strongly relate to your values. These productivity tools are not about doing busy work faster but rather about leading you toward a more purposeful and fulfilling life.

Some of these tools may seem minor, tempting you to brush them off in the belief that they can't possibly make a big difference in your life. The individual impact may be small, but the incremental effect can be quite large. If used over time, each one can have a powerful result. As an example, consider your phone notifications. Have you ever tried to have a conversation with someone over coffee when their (or your) phone was on the table? Even if you both ignore all the beeps, dings, and flashing banners, every small disturbance occupies some space and processing power in your brain, resources that could otherwise be used to stay focused and engage with the person in front of you or to have an innovative idea.

You may think yourself immune from these small distractions, but according to research by Florida State University,[1] they are disruptive even when we consciously choose to ignore them. Despite our best efforts, they cause us to lose focus. When they occur while we're completing a task, they make us more prone to errors. Imagine that you're attempting to focus deeply on something and receive several of these notifications over the course of an hour. Over days, weeks, and years, how much might this time impact your focus, creativity, or work performance or even your ability to have a meaningful conversation?

Many of us believe that we need to be constantly available, but what we seem to gain by responding rapidly to messages can actually be a net loss as we require extra time to repeat actions, repair errors, or explain unclear communication. Extrapolate all that over the long term, and it's easy to see how eliminating microdistractions from our phones could give us back significant chunks of time and lower our stress levels.

Of course, this is only one example. There are many other ways by which we can increase focuse and lower stress, enabling us to do more with less time and effort. This is the ultimate goal of improving our productivity. The Pillar Tool in this chapter, 1.7: Getting Things Done, represents a comprehensive system not only for productivity but also for reducing the stress that often accompanies our efforts to be productive. Let's take a look at it, along with some other tools that will help us to do just that.

---

[1] Florida State University, "Study: Cell phone alerts may be driving you to distraction," College of Arts and Sciences, July 16, 2015, https://artsandsciences.fsu.edu/article/study-cell-phone-alerts-may-be-driving-you-distraction.

Tool 1.1:
What If I Had to Decide Now?

A method for quickly reaching a decision.

Motivation

Sometimes, we go back and forth on making a decision without reaching a definite conclusion because we are unsure about how to resolve our conflicting wants and needs into a cohesive course of action. We're afraid of making the wrong choice, so instead of settling on a decision, we get stuck in limbo, failing to choose at all. At times like this, it can be useful to proactively shift our point of view.

Benefits

- A shift in perspective can be enlightening and galvanize you into action.
- For a simple tool, it can deliver a high return on a small investment of time and energy.

Challenges

- Using this tool can sometimes yield yet another data point to consider, increasing confusion.

Application

If you've been debating several options for a while and can't reach a decision, you can do this experiment. Find a quiet place where you won't be disturbed. Get settled and take a few moments to breathe and relax your mind.

When you're ready, think about the decision you need to make and bring to mind two or more possible solutions. Each option should be very clear and actionable, e.g., "I will talk to X about Y." Then, ask yourself, "If I had to decide *right now*, if I could not change my mind in the future, what would I do?" Continue to sit quietly until the first answer comes to your mind. The answer that comes may or may not ultimately be the right answer for you, but it will surely give you an interesting perspective on what your intuitive mind wants to do. You can take this gut decision at face value or incorporate the information into your deliberations. Either way, hopefully you will gain some valuable information about your desires and thought processes.

This process works for both big life-changing decisions and smaller ones. For example, when you ask, "Do I want to have children?" you may give yourself answers like "I don't know; my job is so demanding," or "I don't know; parenting looks hard." These external factors may have nothing to do with whether you truly *want* to have a child or not. Instead, if you ask yourself, "If I had to decide right now, for forever, with no changing my mind, if I want to have a child, what would I choose?", you may find that a clear *yes* or *no* enters your mind.

You don't need to act on the response right away and, if it's positive, start planning for a child that very minute. Still, the thought process that you go through to reach this conclusion can sometimes reveal deep intuitions that were previously inaccessible and may surprise you, such as "I definitely don't want to go through life without having children." Whatever the outcome of your inquiry, you must still do the hard work of reaching and standing behind a decision, but this process may be easier after you have explored the question from this angle.

Tool 1.2:
Delay Decisions Until the Optimal Moment

Hold off on making decisions for
as long as it's useful (but no longer).

Motivation

Decisions can be hard to make, often because we do not have enough information on hand. We may need to do research or get input from other people before we feel comfortable making a decision. Alternatively, sometimes the information we need simply doesn't exist yet or is not yet concrete (for example, next week's weather). In these instances, it might be best to put off the decision for as long as possible.

Benefits

- You will have more information on which to base your decisions.
- You can postpone nonurgent decisions to a later time to combat decision fatigue.

Challenges

- Sometimes, not making a decision may weigh on your mind and create stress.
- Postponing a decision incurs the cost of remembering to make the decision at a later time.

Application

Sometimes, we're faced with decisions that appear urgent but in fact are not—for example, maybe you're considering making a large purchase or signing a business contract. In these circumstances, you may want to make an immediate decision. Let's say you're buying a new sofa.

What color do you want? Do you want the sprayed-on protection to prevent staining in the event of a spill? What about the upgraded detail on the feet? If you haven't considered these possibilities before going to the furniture shop, you may not know what to pick.

In this case, making an instant decision may have negative consequences. For example, will the fabric protection emit toxic gas, which could trigger migraines in you or your spouse for several weeks? Will it make the fabric feel less soft? Do you eat sitting on your sofa regularly enough for this to be a concern? And does anyone ever pay attention to the detail on the furniture legs?

Unless your existing sofa has completely fallen apart, you may not *need* to make a decision right now. You could go home, think about it, do some research, and ask your friends or family what they think. Maybe, if you wait a month or two, you can passively collect the information you need to make a more informed decision. Passive collection means that you have a subject in the back of your mind—in this example, a new sofa—and set an intention to collect information. You then tune into that frequency, which allows you to pick up on useful information about that subject.

When you tap into the "sofa-buying" frequency, you will suddenly catch a casual office conversation about someone buying a new sofa and liking a particular fabric or spot an article about toxic gas emissions you would otherwise have ignored. This kind of passive information collection is cheap—you don't need to do anything but pay attention—but it can pay off big time by providing you with both more and higher-quality information so you can reach a better decision.

Tool 1.3:
Disconnect

Take time to disengage from your electronic devices and other external interruptions to give your mind a chance to rest or focus.

Motivation

Disconnecting means putting yourself in an interruption-free zone so that you *act* instead of *react*. It's a method of preventing yourself from interacting with people and posts online when it's not urgent. We all have a natural drive that makes us want to respond instantly to notifications as they appear and seek out distractions to avoid being present. However, research shows that frequent distractions increase our stress and decrease our productivity. When we can concentrate without distractions, we are free to focus on what matters most.

Benefits

- Decreases distraction-induced stress.
- Enables you to be more focused and in control of your time.
- Allows you to be present and engaged with life.

Challenges

- Sometimes, responsibilities or obligations require you to be on call, meaning you cannot disconnect.
- At first, the practice may feel awkward, unnecessary, or uncomfortable.

Application

Airplane Mode or Muting

One easy way to disconnect is to switch your phone to airplane mode. This will prevent you from becoming distracted by the numerous notifications. The advantage of using airplane mode over turning off your phone is that it still allows you to easily draft texts and emails, which will be sent when you turn off airplane mode.

If you cannot or will not put your phone in airplane mode, silencing it is another option. This can at least help you partly disconnect. Alternatively, you can turn off the Wi-Fi and data on your phone so that it is essentially silenced, then configure your phone to ring only when certain people call.

Leave Your Phone Behind

To disconnect one step further, you can engage in the full expression of this practice: Leave your phone at home when you go out. By doing so, you free yourself to be completely present with whatever you are doing or whomever you are with, without the temptation to distract yourself with your phone during a dead moment. These moments, when energy drops, can be chances for meditation and useful opportunities for increasing awareness of your surroundings and inner workings.

Another option is to confine your work to a specific work phone. During times when you want to disconnect, leave that phone behind and only take your private phone, of which only select people have the number.

Isolate from Physical Distractions

To fully disconnect, you need to ensure your physical conditions are free of distractions as well. If people, noise, or other physical distractions keep intruding on your work environment, consider moving to a quieter work location or putting a "Do Not Disturb" signal on your desk or office door.

Further Reading

1. Meditation and Vipassana retreats offer other ways to disconnect. They are discussed in the Spirit chapter (Tools 6.1: Meditation and 6.3: Go On a Retreat).

2. Work in Mind Content Team, "One-Third of Office Workers Lack Distraction-Free Spaces," Work in Mind, last updated 2018, https://workinmind.org/2019/01/17/one-third-of-office-workers-lack-distraction-free-spaces/.

Tool 1.4:
The Pomodoro Technique

Work in twenty-five-minute segments.

Motivation

When you're working on something that requires you to concentrate for an extended period of time, such as coding, writing, or analyzing data, you tend to get distracted after a short while. After a brief mental break, you will find it easier to resume focus and return to the task at hand. The Pomodoro Technique encourages you to work this cadence deliberately into your schedule—working for twenty-five minutes, then stopping for five.

When people follow this method, they often report better clarity, higher levels of attentiveness, fewer mistakes, and increased productivity. Structuring distinct work and break times also helps alleviate the urge to escape work because you know a scheduled break is on the way.

Benefits

- Structuring work into short segments encourages stronger focus and higher levels of productivity.
- The expectation of a break helps the brain fight resistance to concentrating on the task at hand.
- Every time you complete twenty-five minutes of work, you feel a sense of achievement, which fuels further productivity.

Challenges

- Some people resist structuring their productive time in the belief that it will feel restrictive.

- Deeper work may require a level of concentration and focus beyond what the Pomodoro Technique can cultivate.

Application

Set a timer for twenty-five minutes. While the timer is running, focus entirely on work; don't engage with distractions such as texting or checking social media. At the end of twenty-five minutes, when you hear the alarm, take a five-minute break to do whatever you feel like—respond to a few emails, take a bathroom break, do a quick meditation. Set your timer to ensure that the break doesn't exceed five minutes. After four twenty-five-minute sessions, take a longer break (fifteen to thirty minutes) to restore your energy and mental sharpness.

Some people find it helpful to stick precisely to the segments dictated by the timer. They stop work even if they are in the middle of a sentence and restart the moment the five minutes are up. Others prefer to give themselves a little flexibility while still maintaining the basic framework.

Digital Pomodoro timers are easy to find, or you can simply use the alarm on your phone. Some people even find it helpful to use a physical timer. At first, the Pomodoro approach can feel rigid, but those who stick with it generally find that it enhances their productivity considerably. You may want to give yourself a few sessions to experiment with it and try to find a rhythm that works for you.

Further Reading

Francesco Cirillo, *The Pomodoro Technique: The Acclaimed Time Management System That Has Transformed How We Work* (Crown Currency, 2018).

Tool 1.5:
Mind Mapping

Clarify your thoughts and break large goals into workable pieces by pouring ideas into a mind map.

Motivation

Our minds are always buzzing with ideas, concepts, and potential solutions to problems. Sometimes, though, we have so much happening in our heads that we cannot *find* or *make sense of* the right ideas, concepts, or solutions when we need them. For example, this often happens when we're faced with a daunting task and don't know where to start or what success looks like. Alternatively, we may find that our minds trouble us at inappropriate times, buzzing with details and questions about various projects on our radars. In these types of situations, mind mapping can be a helpful approach.

Benefits

- Mapping out a task that feels overwhelming can make it more manageable.
- Knowing your thoughts are captured in a trusted system can be reassuring.

Challenges

- Sometimes it's hard to choose between different options for organizing the information you're trying to process.
- Thoroughly mapping out a project and gaining the full benefit of the tool can take some time.

Application

The goal of mind mapping is to pour the contents of your mind into an external format so that the stuff in your head is noted in a way that makes sense to you. This can help you be more creative and expansive in your thoughts. Mind mapping can also help you visualize and drill down into ideas and provides a helpful medium for sharing them with other people.

To generate a mind map, one option is to start with a plain piece of paper and write your end goal or primary topic in the center. Then, all over the paper, start jotting down all your thoughts and ideas about completing your goal or breaking down the central topic. You can draw lines to connect related ideas and concepts. Eventually, you'll create a clear map of your thinking around this project.

Here's an example to help you visualize how this works in practice. Let's say you want to plan an event. There are many different tasks and activities that go into doing this; unless you record them, you can easily forget what you will need to do. To create a mind map, you will begin by writing the event's title (e.g., "My fortieth birthday party") in the center of a piece of paper. Then, you will allow your mind to flow through everything you need to do to plan the event. When a subproject or concept needs clarification, you can zoom into that and add related items.

A popular way to mind map is to use dedicated software or websites. These offer an easy way to electronically organize your mind maps and the ability to focus on parts of the mind map while hiding the irrelevant parts, as well as advanced categorization and search functions. Here's an example of a mind map:

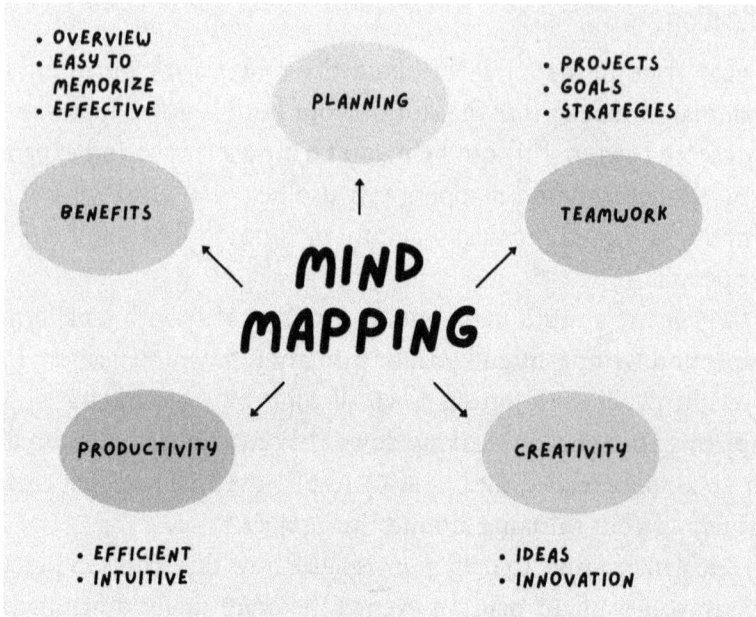

As you can see, a mind map can quickly evolve into an organized reference, containing all the details you will need to consider when planning and holding your event. You can use this map to ensure nothing is left undone or forgotten.

Further Reading

1. To get you started on creating your first mind map, you can use apps like Xmind (https://xmind.app/), which offer templates for many types of projects.

2. SimpleMind (http://simplemind.eu) has full step-by-step directions for creating a mind map.

3. Biggerplate (https://biggerplate.com/) has an assortment of mind-mapping templates.

4. Workflowy (https://workflowy.com/) is a text-based tool that provides a powerful form of mind mapping.

Tool 1.6:
Agenda Documents

Create structured records of subjects you want to discuss with others.

Motivation

Sometimes, it's hard to remember what you wanted to discuss with people. This applies to coworkers, significant others, friends, family members, or even service providers. Agenda documents provide a written record of subjects you'd like to talk about. They give you a document you can easily refer to during a planned or spontaneous meeting to ensure that you remember what you'd like to discuss.

Another advantage of agenda documents is that you can edit them when it might be inefficient or inappropriate to break up the flow of an existing conversation. You can simply make a quick note and return to the discussion. Most of us live busy lives and find it hard to make time for topics we care about. Agenda documents can help bridge this barrier.

Benefits

- Agenda documents provide a space for collecting both big ideas and small yet important details.
- Making agenda documents helps you stay focused and calm, knowing you have made a note of key concepts and will come back to them.
- When you use agenda documents with your teams, everyone involved will know what they missed during meetings.

Challenges

- Might require buy-in from other people you want to use them with, especially if you decide to make the documents shared and collaborative.
- In certain situations, especially non-work scenarios, using agenda documents could feel artificial.

Application

Fundamentally, an agenda document is any list of items you want to discuss with someone. Each time a new topic you know you'd like to discuss at some point pops into your head,, add it to the list. Whenever you have an uninterrupted conversation with the person in question, simply open the document. Everything you want to talk about will be listed in front of you.

If you prefer, you can make agenda documents shared so that others can add and edit items. In these circumstances, cloud-based note-taking apps, such as Google Docs, are very useful. Another option is to keep them in a dedicated WhatsApp group where everyone is notified whenever an item is added. The important factor is to reach an agreement about a tool that works for everyone. Or, failing that, agree that each person will use their own preferred method and bring their own list to the meeting.

There are two types of agenda documents:

- **Live agenda doc:** To create a live agenda doc, simply add items as they arise, then remove them once they're discussed. As items are cleared, these documents empty out, showing you what remains to be discussed.
- **Rolling agenda doc:** A rolling agenda document includes a "next meeting" section at the top of the document where you add relevant items. After each meeting, note the current date, process these agenda items, and open a new section for the upcoming

meeting; this makes it easy to add new items. This kind of document is often valuable for team meetings, as it both captures the history of your discussions and allows for conversations about fresh topics. You can share the document with team members, inviting everyone to add topics that need to be discussed at the next meeting, along with their names so everyone knows who wants to discuss which subject.

Agenda documents can be useful not only in business contexts but also in personal ones. However, understand that the idea of creating an agenda for personal relationships can generate resistance. Some people will immediately recognize that it's a method of staying synchronized and maximizing the quality of your conversations, whereas others will push back on the basis that it lacks spontaneity and feels emotionally cold to bring an agenda to personal conversations.

Depending on the context, it might be best to have an honest conversation on why you want to try this tool, then agree on a way of doing it that's comfortable for the other person. For example, you might try keeping your agenda document separately and referring to it before meeting the other person but not looking at it openly while you're together.

Tool 1.7:
⫘ Getting Things Done

The art of stress-free productivity.

Motivation

The Getting Things Done (GTD) methodology was created by David Allen and described in his book *Getting Things Done: The Art of Stress-Free Productivity*.[2] It's a system for creating order and clarity in your mind. The GTD process involves dumping all nonessential information out of your brain, organizing your actions into projects, and systematically executing these projects.

You can use this tool to create more clarity, order, and control in your work and personal life. By building and regularly reviewing an inventory of your commitments to yourself and others, you gain a sense of trust and calm. This allows you more freedom and spontaneity: When you have a clear picture of your projects, you're free at any moment to prioritize what's important to you, be it a work meeting, spending time with your kids, or just taking a nap.

Benefits

- Increased productivity, order, and sense of control.
- Lower stress levels and less wasted effort.
- Easy to get started without a huge learning curve.

Challenges

- It takes time and effort to fully master GTD.
- Expect that you will fall off the wagon at times.

---

[2] David Allen, *Getting Things Done: The Art of Stress-Free Productivity* (Penguin Books, 2002).

Application

GTD is an all-encompassing methodology; this section is only a brief summary of it. In order to get the full benefits, you should read Allen's book or check out other online resources and courses.

At the core of GTD is a workflow system of five stages:

1. **Capture: Collect what has your attention.**

   Get information out of your head and pour it into an inbox. This frees you from nagging thoughts such as "Gotta buy groceries" and lets you process them at the appropriate time.

2. **Clarify: Process what it means.**

   Turn each inbox item into a meaningful, clear action. If you noted down "groceries," for example, you might change it to "Buy groceries: two gallons of milk, ten eggs, and four bananas." For every item, make sure you define a concrete physical step you can take to advance this action or project. If you can't find anything you need to do with the information, either file it for future reference or trash it.

3. **Organize: Put it where it belongs.**

   If you can perform an action in two minutes or less, do it now. (Allen calls this the two-minute rule). Otherwise, you can do one of several things: Delegate it; file it as an action or a project; defer it to a later date; or, if you're not committed to completing it soon, perhaps move it into a folder labeled "someday/maybe."

4. **Reflect: Review frequently.**

   Periodically, take time to review your projects, actions, and everything else that needs your attention. This helps you prioritize important actions instead of just putting out the hottest and most urgent fires. By doing so, you can build a holistic workflow that takes care of a range of tasks, from buying milk and answering your boss's emails, to planning big life changes such as moving or switching jobs or careers, to answering questions like, "Where do I want to be in five to ten years?" You can do this at multiple regular intervals, e.g., every week, month, or year, according to your needs.

5. Engage: Simply do.

Finally, you have to just buy the damn milk or answer that email.

The following are a few examples of handy GTD techniques that you can use right off the bat:

Mind Sweep

A mind sweep is a way to clear information from your brain and move it into a trusted system, freeing up your brain to focus on other activities. Sit down with a piece of paper (or a computer, phone, or other device), and take stock of what is on your mind: the things you need to do; the conversations you need to have; the resources you need to find; the questions you need answered; and so forth.

Write every item down as a separate bullet point; each of these items will go into your inbox to be processed at a later time. Don't worry about listing too many tasks. At this stage, writing something down doesn't commit you to doing anything about it. When you clarify and organize this list, you can decide to trash some items.

There are various kinds of mind sweeps. You can do a quick one-minute sweep at the beginning of your day. You can do a full twenty-minute sweep across various categories, such as health and vitality, significant other, work, finances, and so forth. You can focus on a particular field or problem; for example, mind sweep while walking around your house and note down everything you'd like to repair or improve about it.

A mind sweep differs from a mind map (see Tool 1.5: Mind Mapping), which is geared toward helping you gather all your thoughts about a concept or goal in one place and mapping the connections between them. Mind sweeping is less concerned with grouping or cataloging thoughts. It is more a method of clearing your mind in a way that frees you from conscious or unconscious worries. Once you have written everything down in a safe place where your brain knows it can access it, your mind will be clearer and more readily able to focus on a specific task or be creative.

Two-Minute Rule

The two-minute rule is briefly described above. It is simple: when you are organizing an action in your system, ask yourself whether you can complete this action in under two minutes. If so, do it immediately. If not, add it to a list of actions to do later or delegate it to someone.

It's important to estimate correctly. Some tasks may appear to be achievable in one or two minutes but instead blow up to ten or more, leaving you asking, "What was I just doing and why?" Like most things, your accuracy will improve with time and practice. One way to train your estimations is to keep a physical two-minute timer handy and check your guesses against the timer.

Inbox Zero

While inbox zero was not created by David Allen, it was inspired by GTD, then integrated into it. Many of us have thousands of read and unread messages in our email inboxes. But, according to Allen, that's not the role of an inbox. An inbox is not meant to store things forever. It's meant as a place for things to arrive, be processed, and move out of, just like the physical inbox where your mailman leaves letters.

Usually, if you're on top of things, you don't keep your letters in your mailbox for a year. You take them out of the mailbox and do something with them. You read them, toss them, file what needs storing, and make room for more items. The same can be said for your email. You can process your email using the five stages of GTD to keep it down to zero messages, or at least a minimal number. If you can do this, you'll find your inbox is less stressful to open and more efficient to process. The general rule here is that *you should open and read an email only once*, rather than reading and rereading the same emails and subject lines. Besides, your inbox is prettier when it's empty.

Review

Reviews—revisiting and optimizing different areas of your workflow, including your GTD workflow—are an important part of GTD. You can schedule reviews for specific times: daily, weekly, monthly, quarterly, yearly, or whenever fits your life best. Each one can be tailored to your particular circumstances and needs and will usually address one particular horizon of focus. Allen describes six horizons:

5. Purpose: Solve the world's overpopulation problem.
4. Vision: Establish a civilization on Mars.
3. Goals and Objectives: Find a way to reuse rockets shipped to space.
2. Areas of Focus: Establish a rocket team.
1. Projects: Hire Max from NASA.
0. Action: Call John to get Max's phone number.

While you can approach these horizons bottom-up or top-down, most people find it easiest to first tackle horizons 0 and 1 with daily and weekly reviews. These clear up time and energy, allowing you to address higher horizons.

What should you review? There are numerous possibilities, including your different inboxes; your projects; the someday/maybe list; the contents of your calendar; and anything else pulling at your attention. To illustrate this, let's look at a daily review.

Each morning, you can spend a few minutes deciding on your focus for the day and the most important task you want to accomplish. You can use this time to clear various inboxes—such as texts, emails, notifications, and physical letters—depending on your life and work style. If you keep a decision log (see Tool 1.9: Log Your Life), you can review it and, if you haven't already, update it with every major decision you made the day before.

You can also make a calendar review part of your daily review. You can go over the day before, the current day, and the next day, and look for anything that requires action. Maybe you want to send a follow-up email about a recent business meeting or text a friend you met yesterday and share how much fun you had with her. Or you might want to look at tomorrow's schedule and eliminate any double bookings you've made—and make sure you have time for lunch! Of course, if you discover any actions that you need to take based on this information, you can add these to your inbox.

A key part of your daily review, or any other review, is to experiment and customize it to your particular needs. You can also use the weekly or monthly reviews to think about and customize the structure of your daily review. A review is a checkpoint—it's an opportunity for you to zoom out of your current horizon of focus and change your perspective.

Further Reading

1. The Getting Things Done website: https://gettingthingsdone. com/.

2. Sample daily & weekly review templates on Workflowy: https:// workflowy.com/s/gtd-review-lists/PhDOt9Q7YHEiYfon.

3. Mindsweep template on Trello: https://trello.com/c/BZJOOTR6.

Tool 1.8:
Brainstorming

Explore many potential solutions to a problem.

Motivation

Sometimes you encounter a tough problem and are unsure how to make progress. You could be faced with a goal you don't know how to reach or be seeking an innovative approach to a conundrum you've approached previously. Brainstorming can open your mind to other aspects of the problem at hand, helping you look at the problem in a novel way and come up with an original way to tackle it.

Benefits

- Brainstorming can be a valuable way to access solutions that are unavailable in normal modes of thinking.
- Generates a large number of potential solutions rapidly, possibly uncovering better alternatives to other methods.

Challenges

- It can be hard to resist self-censorship, which will limit the benefit of this technique.

Application

Brainstorming is simple. All you need is a goal you wish to reach or a problem you are trying to solve, along with a way of recording your inspirations (usually a notebook or digital equivalent). With the goal or problem in mind, simply write down all the ideas that come to your mind, even those that appear silly or impossible.

It's important to let even implausible notions flow. This opens your mind to creative solutions, inviting you to keep brainstorming until you hit something that works. If you censor yourself from proposing a particular solution, a part of your brain will continue to ruminate on it. By writing down even possibilities that are obviously irrelevant, you free up your mind to process other ideas in rapid succession. Stay with the process for a set period of time or until you have written down a predetermined number of potential solutions (for example, ten minutes or twelve ideas). Even thoughts that initially appear ridiculous may contain a spark of inspiration that can be later adapted into a practical solution.

You can brainstorm alone or in a group. In a group, the same principle applies: At this stage, it's essential not to critique or criticize other people's contributions. Simply write them down. To be effective, brainstorming must be a safe space where people are encouraged to bring even crazy ideas to the table in pursuit of truly creative insights.

After you've completed the brainstorming process, look again at your list and start to consider which solutions might work, perhaps with some modifications. You may wish to vote on ideas and concentrate on those the group believes have the most merit, narrowing your options until you reach something you can act upon.

Further Reading

1. Hal Gregerson, "Better Brainstorming," *Harvard Business Review,* March 1, 2018, https://hbr.org/2018/03/better-brainstorming.
2. Team Asana, "29 Brainstorming Techniques for Creativity," Asana, February 4, 2024, https://asana.com/resources/brainstorming-techniques.

Tool 1.9:
Log Your Life

Record major decisions for later review.

Motivation

Creating a decision log allows you to record and reflect on both the decisions you make as well as their consequences, enabling you to make better decisions in the future. By tracking what you choose to do and the outcomes of your choices, you set yourself up to learn valuable lessons and make future decisions from a more informed place.

Benefits

- The act of stopping to record a decision gives it more weight and allows you to course correct if needed.
- A structured review of past decisions and their outcomes can help you calibrate your internal compass toward more beneficial choices.

Challenges

- The added bureaucracy can be burdensome if applied too widely.

Application

Create a document recording the date you made a decision, what you chose, and why you made it. You may also want to add space for comments about the consequences or any other relevant info. You can update this log in real time, following significant developments, or spend a few minutes each week reflecting on recent major decisions you've taken.

The next step is to integrate a review process to assess past decisions. You can do this on a monthly or quarterly cadence and observe not just decisions but also their outcomes. Ideally, you will create a feedback loop where you'll record your decisions and then take the time to assess their consequences on a regular basis. This review informs and improves your future decisions. As you repeat this process, you build on the insights gleaned from each iteration of the decision review process, thereby making better and better decisions.

Further Reading

Erik Larson, "Avoid Decision-Making Mistakes - Start A Decision Log," *Forbes,* last updated June 22, 2017, https://forbes.com/sites/eriklarson/2017/06/20/build-up-decisive-work-habits-start-a-decision-log/.

Tool 1.10:
Default to Openness

Be more transparent in your communication and only opt for privacy if there's a concrete reason to do so.

Motivation

Most people default to a superficial communication style and only share what's truly on their minds with one or two close friends or colleagues. They feel that openness is something to be avoided unless absolutely necessary, and they wait for a good reason to open up. Until they have one, they keep their cards close to their chests, missing out on many opportunities to connect with others, feel heard, and try new things.

Flipping this philosophy means choosing transparency by default and trusting and sharing with others (unless they demonstrate that they are not to be trusted). This attitude can tremendously enrich quality of life and relationships and expose people to serendipitous opportunities that would have been impossible to predict otherwise. Like all tools, this tool isn't meant for every person and situation and should be used consciously.

Benefits

- Offers a richer, more alive way to communicate with others.
- Enhances life with opportunities to connect, learn, teach, and even inspire others.
- Opening up to people will naturally encourage them to reciprocate.

Challenges

- Opening up involves being vulnerable, which can sometimes lead to emotional pain.

- Being transparent without accidentally oversharing can sometimes be tricky. Failing to walk this line skilfully can hurt other people and your relationships.

Application

To make the most of this tool, it's important to be honest with yourself and others (see Tool 2.7: Radical Honesty).

This tool is about flipping the switch on your mode of communication. Instead of defaulting to not sharing information and only doing so when there is a compelling reason, you can acquire the habit of sharing freely and only hitting the brakes when it becomes necessary. Transparency is not a binary setting of either not sharing anything with anyone or sharing everything with everyone. Rather, you can take a gradual path to opening up and experiment until you find a level that works for you.

As you open up and default to sharing, make sure your sharing choices match your overall preferences and well-being. Despite this new inclination to share, there may be situations in which you don't want to share an intimate truth. Just remember that saying "I don't want to talk about it" is a valid reply.

Opening up sometimes comes with a price. Some people won't welcome your free and uninvited sharing or simply won't know how to respond. They may be accustomed to superficial chatter and lack the capacity for deeper conversations. When this happens, it's good feedback. You might end up losing some relationships but discovering closer and more meaningful ones in their stead.

Tool 1.11:
Celebrate Success

Take the time to appreciate and celebrate
your accomplishments.

Motivation

Life is more than just work, work, work. Highly productive people sometimes feel that they must always be doing something; many complete one project only to immediately move on to the next. Frequently, these people become so stressed about completing projects, absorbing important information, ticking off tasks, and meeting deadlines that they forget to stop, breathe, and smell the roses.

This endless treadmill of productivity can lead to burnout and generate ever-increasing stress. Furthermore, those who stake their emotional well-being on the successful completion of a project can become disappointed, even despondent, if they fail to achieve their aims. Celebrating successes of any size can help people enjoy the journey, not just the outcome.

Benefits

- Celebrations remind us that achievement alone can't deliver true well-being and that sharing enjoyable experiences with loved ones is also essential to happiness.

- When you celebrate what you've already achieved, you boost your motivation to accomplish even more.

- Many people think negatively about themselves and their lives. Bringing successes into focus can counter this tendency.

Challenges

- If you're highly stressed, celebrating your successes might feel disingenuous or meaningless.

- There may be times when other obligations take precedence over celebrations, distracting from them and diluting their positive impact.

Application

Celebrating is about appreciating what you have accomplished. You may wish to do this when you hit a specific project milestone or simply when you reach the end of a challenging day, week, or year. The reason is less important than the ritual itself.

The actual celebration can be as large or small as you wish. Pausing for a few seconds to breathe and reflect with pride on your progress is a celebration, as is taking a walk while listening to a favorite song and eating some ice cream. If you are part of a team, you can include them, too, or share your wins with close friends or loved ones.

Another celebratory habit is to spend a few minutes before you go to bed each night reflecting on your successes from the day. This can be a particularly useful method to reduce stress and build a sense of self-worth. To take this even further, try writing down what you're celebrating, either digitally or with pen and paper.

This is similar to doing a daily gratitude practice (see Tool 3.3: Gratitude) but with a slightly different focus. Gratitude can focus on anything: yourself; others; nature; the world at large. Your successes, however, are your personal accomplishments. Celebrating them is a reminder of your abilities and the effort you put into reaching your goals.

Further Reading

1. ET Bureau, "Boost These Hormones to Succeed as a Leader at Work," *The Economic Times*, last updated December 10, 2018, https://economictimes.indiatimes.com/wealth/earn/boost-these-hormones-to-succeed-as-a-leader-at-work/articleshow/66988190.cms.

2. Jodi Clarke, "Healthy Ways to Celebrate Success," VerywellMind, last updated October 6, 2021, https://verywellmind.com/healthy-ways-to-celebrate-success-4163887.

Tool 1.12:
Pause and Ask Why

Reconnect with the reasons why you're doing what you're doing.

Motivation

Sometimes, you may get too invested in completing tasks (either pre-planned or ongoing). This can result in a fake productivity loop that feels very active and gratifying but in reality may be ineffective, not unlike running on a hamster wheel. You may feel quite productive, but you're not necessarily moving in the right direction. The task you're working on might not be relevant anymore, either absolutely or compared to other more important things you could be working on.

Benefits

- Spend energy on the activities most important to you.
- Reduce procrastination and busy work.

Challenges

- The dopamine rush of completing tasks might lure you toward low-priority activities.
- We are often action driven, with a natural tendency to solve the problems in front of us rather than ask ourselves, "Is this the right problem to solve right now?"
- The highest-priority challenges on your agenda are often more difficult, tempting you to avoid them.

Application

On an ongoing basis, while working on your projects, take time to pause and simply ask yourself: "Why am I doing this? Why is this important to me? What will be made possible if this is done?" Give yourself a few seconds to answer (optionally, write it down). This allows you to shift your frame of thinking so that you can see the bigger picture and compare this project with other things you could do with your time or energy.

This doesn't have to be a long process—even a few seconds of thought gives you an opportunity to rise above the automatic level of action and connect with a higher self that's more aware of your priorities. If you want to internalize this habit, you may want to do this regularly, at daily/weekly intervals, or whenever you start a project.

Should you discover conflicts between the priorities of your higher self and the instant gratification sought by your automatic self, you have an opportunity to let the two sides talk it through (see Tool 3.4: Talk to Your Inner Selves). Achieving meaningful things usually involves some inescapable difficulty, so you may want to embrace that.

Further Reading

Simon Sinek, *Start with Why: How Great Leaders Inspire Everyone to Take Action* (Portfolio, 2011).

Tool 1.13:
Accountability Partners

Hold yourself accountable to others for your commitments.

Motivation

When working alone, it can often be hard to stay on task and stick to a desired schedule or commitment. One way to boost your determination is to connect with an accountability partner with whom you share your goals and progress. Knowing that you will report your achievements to someone else provides a motivation boost to do your best.

You can apply this approach to almost any aspect of your life, from becoming more productive at work, to watching what you eat, to giving up smoking, to exercising regularly, or even to communicating more effectively with your spouse.

Benefits

- Reporting your progress to another person, knowing that they're emotionally invested in your success, can be an excellent way to stay on track.
- Helps you feel connected to others even when performing solitary tasks.

Challenges

- If you don't choose your partner wisely, you may find that they don't provide you with the support you need.
- An accountability partner is not a substitute for your own determination to make positive changes in your life.

Application

There are numerous ways to locate and work with an accountability partner. One of the easiest is to go into environments where you are likely to meet other people who are working solo, such as coworking spaces. Some may have bulletin boards or online communities where you can search for an accountability partner. Another option is to approach a friend or spouse and invite them to connect with you in this way.

Once you have found someone suitable, you need to decide how you will track your mutual progress. You may choose to update one another only when you are *in accountability*—doing what you committed to do—or only when you're *out of accountability* and miss your targets. If you prefer, you could schedule a weekly check-in on your goals when you each reflect and review on the past week.

Some people find value in connecting with others who are united by a similar focus, which could be anything from dieting to dating to performing stand-up comedy, and reporting regularly on their progress. If the activity is something you can do together—for example, working out at the gym—you can take advantage of this to boost your commitment. Neither of you will want to disappoint the other, so it's more likely you will both show up.

A topical accountability buddy (or group of buddies) can be a powerful ally. Another option is to use an app that tracks your progress. You can log your results from day to day or week to week, or you can compete against other people for extra motivation. Whichever option you choose, it's important that you're clear on your goals and share them with your partner so that you can assess how far you've moved toward them. Naturally, it's also crucial to be honest; lying to yourself or your partner will undermine the process and limit the value of this approach.

Further Reading

Use Focusmate to help you find an accountability partner: https://focusmate.com.

Tool 1.14:
If You See a Job, It's Yours

If you recognize that something needs to be done, take responsibility for doing it.

Motivation

It is easy and comforting to complain about problems and feel upset that other people aren't doing their jobs properly. However, neither complaining nor being upset resolves anything. Taking action, or otherwise initiating a solution, can both fix the problem at hand and alleviate negative emotions, as well as inspire others to be proactive about tackling problems they see.

Benefits

- Fixing things can be empowering for you and inspiring for others.
- It's better to take action and address problems than blame others for what isn't getting done.

Challenges

- Not *every* problem can be yours to solve. If this culture becomes too ingrained, you may become inhibited from mentioning any issue you can't immediately fix.

Application

The fundamental principle here is that if you see something that's wrong, broken, or problematic but that can be fixed, it will be more empowering for you to step up and take action than to become frustrated or neglect the issue. At Burning Man, this concept is considered so important that it is enshrined in the event's principles of radical self-reliance and participation.

Not every problem is immediately fixable. In some cases, you may be able to enact the solution yourself. In others, you may need to advocate for action, doing whatever you can to push a resolution forward. Whichever option you choose, take ownership of the situation and find solutions to turn it around, or recruit others to work on solutions with you. Living and working in a culture where everyone adopts this approach can be incredibly refreshing. Instead of complaining about what's wrong, people get in the habit of making things better. It can also be contagious: When people witness others confidently taking responsibility and actively seeking solutions, they are more likely to do the same.

Further Reading

"The 10 Principles of Burning Man," Burning Man Project, https://burningman.org/culture/philosophical-center/10-principles/.

Tool 1.15:
Declutter Your Space

Clear your field of bothersome distractions.

Motivation

As mentioned in Disconnect (Tool 1.3), even brief challenges to your focus will eat into your capacity to be productive—or to simply enjoy life. A cluttered visual or auditory field can easily take a toll on your mental processes, slowing you down.

Distraction takes many forms. Whether you have extra tabs open on your computer desktop or clutter on your physical desk, extraneous stuff provides a visual interruption to your thoughts, draining your energy. In the same way, hearing beeps, clicks, and other notifications from your phone can divert your attention toward meaningless tasks. If you're feeling drained, scattered, or just not productive enough because you're having difficulty concentrating, it may help to do whatever you can to eliminate distractions.

Benefits

- Reduces or eliminates mental drain.
- Helps you stay focused on your priorities.
- A clean, quiet environment can be more enjoyable.

Challenges

- We may become emotionally attached to familiar objects or even comforted by phone notifications and find it hard to remove them.
- The benefits aren't immediately felt, so this is often underprioritized.

Application

Take some time to arrange your physical environment so that it provides minimal distraction. Photographs and empty coffee cups take up space in your thinking. Clear your desktop and desk of unnecessary items and mess by sorting things into appropriate folders or drawers, storing them somewhere, or trashing them.

The same applies to your online environment. Hide or close browser tabs, icons, or extensions. Uninstall any unused apps and consider adding a monthly or quarterly reminder to declutter your phone. Alter your settings so that you receive fewer notifications and so that those you do receive are in a less distracting form—for example, silent rather than a vibration or a noise.

Removing distractions will make it easier to be productive when you want to be. It will also make your spaces more pleasant and enjoyable to relax in. A cluttered space can provoke worry and the subtle sense that you need to do something to tidy it, even when you're trying to wind down. An uncluttered space is a pleasure to inhabit.

You may not be sure how to determine which objects are important to you. One way to choose is to invoke the KonMari Method. Put simply, she asks whether items spark joy. Those that do can remain; those that do not can be removed or recycled.

Further Reading

1. Explore the KonMari method: https://konmari.com/.
2. "Why Is It Important to Declutter?" Forest Homes, https://foresthomesstore.com/blogs/decor-for-wellbeing/why-is-it-important-to-declutter-how-can-it-benefit-your-mental-health-and-others-wellbeing.

Tool 1.16:
Allow Yourself to Rest

Take a break from endless productivity.

Motivation

In modern society, it sometimes seems like we value productivity above all else. This can become exhausting, ultimately leading to burnout or even total breakdown. To balance this bias toward productivity, it's important to give yourself permission to take a break every now and then.

Ultimately, life is about more than what we create, and some of the most important elements of being human can't be measured and optimized. By taking an occasional break from the pressure to produce, you can open up space to nurture relationships with yourself and others and feel more complete and rounded.

Benefits

- Nourish the capacity to be present and experience a non-goal-oriented approach to reality.
- Often, we're more creative following a period of rest and recharging.

Challenges

- We may feel guilty about not achieving enough or fear missing deadlines if we take time off.

Application

In a world that seems to be constantly pressuring us to do more, we often find that the only way to secure free time is to give ourselves permission to schedule it into our calendars.

Choose a date (maybe a recurring weekly or monthly slot in your calendar) and block out at least a couple of hours. Decide not to schedule anything during this time; simply allow yourself to rest and rejuvenate.

How exactly you do this is up to you. You may wish to set a timer and meditate, which can be very refreshing (see Tool 6.1: Meditation). Alternatively, you may enjoy taking a walk, napping, or calling a friend to chat about whatever you feel like. Some people enjoy exercising or playing a social sport. If this is you, be sure you're approaching these activities with the mindset of taking time off, as opposed to pushing yourself to succeed.

While none of these activities are directly productive, ironically, you may find that when you do return to work, you'll be both physically and mentally refreshed, with a clearer mind and a greater drive to succeed.

Tool 1.17:
Atomic Habits

Strategies for establishing and maintaining new habits.

Motivation

When you choose to start a new habit, such as exercising or practicing a skill that you wish to develop, it's easy to lose motivation and quit before you truly establish it as part of your routine. You may forget your intention as you get busy or let it slip down your list of priorities when other things come up. When you already have a busy life, it can be tough to fit new behaviors into your existing schedule. If you're committed to making your new habit work, however, try the techniques popularized by *Atomic Habits* author James Clear. They are designed specifically to make it as easy as possible to positively alter your habits.

Benefits

- Provides a comprehensive recipe for adopting positive, helpful habits.
- Taps into our natural drives, reducing the need to rely on willpower.

Challenges

- Setting up your environment to support new habits takes thought and discipline.
- No matter how easy you make it to adopt new habits, you'll still need some commitment to make them work.

Application

James Clear's book, *Atomic Habits*, has become a best-selling phenomenon.[3] In it, he distills the factors that create positive behavioral change

---

[3] James Clear, *Atomic Habits* (Avery, 2018).

into a few simple rules and encourages readers to leverage these rules when adopting new habits. In order, they are:

- Make it obvious.
- Make it attractive.
- Make it easy.
- Make it satisfying.

Let's walk through these in turn. To make it obvious, create visuals or other reminders of whatever you want to do so that you can't overlook it. Let's say you want to start running in the morning. You could place Post-it notes on the fridge, by the front door, and on your bedroom table, reminding you that you plan to get out and go for a run at a particular time.

To make a habit attractive, the idea is to give yourself every opportunity to say yes to it, perhaps by pairing new habits with existing ones you already enjoy. In the running example, you might choose to put headphones on and play music or a podcast you enjoy while you run. Alternatively, maybe you have a habit of visiting a park in the early morning and feeding the birds. If you choose to run to the park, you can pair those habits together in your mind, making it more likely you'll keep up with your new habit.

Making it easy is about reducing the friction that prevents you from moving forward. To get yourself out the door and on a run, you might prepare your running clothes and shoes the night before and leave your coffee and a snack out on the kitchen table so you don't need to waste a moment thinking about them when you get up and possibly succumb to the temptation to go back to bed. The shoes could also double as a reminder instead of a note.

Finally, to make it satisfying, intensify the habit loop by celebrating small victories and finding ways to make your new habit feel rewarding. For example, try tracking your progress by ticking off days on a calendar or by writing details of your runs in an app or on paper so that you can see yourself running faster or farther. Another option is to create a reward system in which you allow yourself treats, such as a massage or a fun date night with your partner, when you achieve goals, such as running four days per week. It's important that the reward doesn't counteract the habit—in this case, a big slice of cake might not be a great reward for maintaining your running habit. Finally, consider talking to friends, family, or a supportive community about your goals so that you have the satisfaction of sharing your achievements with them and gaining social reinforcement.

Each of these principles works in reverse if there's an existing habit you wish to eliminate. Let's say you eat too many cookies. You can make it invisible by hiding the cookies at the back of the cupboard or, even better, not keeping them in the house at all. Make it unattractive by concentrating on the weight gain and negative health consequences of eating cookies, not the delicious taste. Make it difficult by telling your partner you wish to eat fewer cookies and agreeing to pay a fine if you exceed your desired intake (see Tool 1.13: Accountability Partners).

Finally, make it unsatisfying by linking a failure to achieve your goal with negative outcomes. This isn't about punishing yourself for perceived failures—it's about finding ways to hold yourself accountable. For example, you might publicly commit to a goal, knowing that you will need to share your progress, including any setbacks, with others. You could even use an app that donates money to causes you dislike in the event that you don't reach your goals. These approaches harness your natural aversion to loss, creating an environment where the desire to avoid negative feedback helps you stay disciplined and on track.

Clear's *Atomic Habits* methods have proven successful for millions of people, enabling them to develop more positive habits and reduce negative ones. While it's true that it takes time to solidify a new habit, once anchored, habits become significantly easier to sustain.

Further Reading

1. "Atomic Habits: How to get 1% Better Every Day": https://youtube.com/watch?time_continue=2&v=U_nzqnXWvSo&embeds_referring_euri=https%3A%2F%2Fjamesclear.com%2F&source_ve_path=Mjg2NjY.

CHAPTER TWO

RELATIONSHIPS

"Trust is built in very small moments, which I call 'sliding door' moments. In any interaction, there is a possibility of connecting with your partner or turning away from your partner."

—John Gottman

Relationships are one of the most important aspects of life. In fact, numerous studies have suggested that the quality of our relationships is the most crucial factor in determining our happiness. The cornerstone of all relationships is effective communication, but unfortunately, not all of us grow up with successful models for forming satisfying relationships. While some of us may see the adults around us modeling healthy behaviors from an early age, thus receiving a roadmap for effective communication, others may learn from role models that the way to deal with our emotions is to shout, sulk, or drink alcohol, strategies that we repeat as we grow older. Without learning and absorbing good relational practices when we're young, we have to learn better ways through trial and error, which can often be a long and painful road.

In these circumstances, we may struggle to know what we want in relationships, then struggle even more to maintain them. We may have difficulty working through conflict, understanding ourselves and others, and managing our emotions.

If you're experiencing some difficulties in your relationships—and most of us are—the following tools may be of assistance. Each one is designed to help you interact better with both other people and with yourself. They cover a range of situations, from romantic partnerships to conversations with family members to interactions with virtual strangers (e.g., at a new job or a dinner party where you don't know anyone). Whatever the scenario, these tools provide ways to connect, interact, and avoid and resolve conflicts. They will help you understand the reasons why you habitually express yourself the way you do, assist you in gaining clarity about the motivations and needs of others, and offer new ways of breaking down barriers between you and those you care about.

Several of the tools in this section deal with the nuances of relating intimately with another person. They provide insight into figuring out what kinds of relationships you want in your life, along with methods for improving the relationships you're already in—for example, how to address consent and share your emotions vulnerably and honestly.

Sometimes the best form of communication is silence—whether in the form of listening with intention or in the form of giving yourself and another person some emotional space to process events or arguments. The tools here acknowledge this with some aimed at helping you utilize these softer modes of communication. Equally, there are tools to facilitate better verbal or written expression.

This chapter includes a Pillar Tool, 2.1: Nonviolent Communication, which is where we'll begin our list.

Tool 2.1:
▯ Nonviolent Communication

A compassionate approach to relating to yourself and others based on feelings and needs.

Nonviolent Communication (NVC), created by Dr. Marshall Rosenberg, is an approach to relationships that views *feelings* and *needs* as the basic drivers of all human behavior.[4] It encourages us to move away from automatic patterns of behavior to get what we want and instead connect first on the level of feelings and needs. Connecting in this way can open us up to new options and enable us to act in ways that will better meet everyone's needs as well as build more harmonious relationships.

The core assumption of NVC is that all humans are driven by the same basic feelings and needs, which come alive within us at different times in our lives. With NVC, needs are universal, often described by a single word—for example, sustenance, freedom, safety, sexual expression, love, rest, space, quiet, and many more. When our needs are fulfilled, we are satisfied and experience pleasant feelings like calm, inspiration, appreciation, confidence, or relief. When a need is unmet, however, we experience unpleasant feelings such as fear, sadness, anger, anxiety, or exhaustion. Instead of suppressing these negative emotions, we can explore them and discover the needs behind them, which allows us to attempt to meet them.

Our needs drive our feelings, which in turn drive our behavior. Our feelings push us to choose strategies that we hope will meet our needs and thus stop unhappy feelings and bring about pleasant feelings. Usually, this happens at an unconscious level, and we are unaware of both the needs and feelings that drive us. When we get in

---

[4] Marshall B. Rosenberg, *Nonviolent Communication: A Language of Life* (Puddle Dancer Press, 2015).

touch with our feelings and needs, we open up to new strategies that can better meet everyone's needs or to existing strategies that previously seemed unworkable.

Motivation

When people feel disconnected from themselves or others (at work, within personal relationships, etc.), they often feel emotional pain and emptiness. They may want to live more authentically, express themselves more deeply, or experience more love, freedom, and safety in their lives. NVC helps us achieve deeper and more fulfilling connections with ourselves and others and transform conflicts into win-win scenarios.

Benefits

- NVC allows people to forge deeper connections by encouraging them to connect via universal feelings and needs.
- By focusing on underlying needs instead of arguing over specific ways of action (strategies), fresh, creative solutions naturally arise.
- You can use NVC to connect with yourself and identify and fully experience your feelings and needs, which can have therapeutic value.
- NVC helps you replace fear, shame, and judgment with acceptance, compassion, and an open heart.

Challenges

- NVC differs so much from the ways many have been taught to relate to the world that it can feel alien or utopic. It can take a while to feel comfortable using NVC.
- Beginners to NVC often sound mechanical, and it can take a while for practitioners to integrate its essence while retaining a pattern of speech that sounds natural.

- Newcomers to NVC often try to force it down people's throats, which can be very off-putting and counterproductive.

Application

NVC is a broad approach with many different applications. It can help people live more fulfilling, connected lives, as well as connect them to themselves and other people.

According to NVC, every person is always trying to meet their needs. Conflict arises when one or more people believe that one of their needs is threatened by the needs or actions of another. In fact, people are usually unaware of their needs and instead insist on implementing a particular strategy without understanding what deeper needs that strategy serves for them. In these situations, people often miss strategies that would better meet everyone's needs and instead have tunnel vision on one or two readily available strategies.

NVC suggests that we practice awareness of our interpretations and judgments and try to base our communication with others on concrete observations. One way to do this is to find something objective in the physical world that both parties can agree on. When we stop focusing on judgments and who is at fault and instead focus on how we can agree on facts, we can move the conversation toward empathy. When we're not attached to specific strategies, we can move from making demands to true requests that respect the other's autonomy, accepting the possibility that the other person may refuse our requests.

With practice, we can learn to see and empathize with one another's needs, which helps us connect. From a connected place, it's easier to look for a peaceful solution together. Below is an example of how to use NVC for conflict resolution, but it can be useful in a wide variety of situations.

Let's say a woman comes home late from work and is disappointed to find a sink full of dirty dishes. Her husband has been caring for their kids all day and is glad she's home because he wants her to wash the dishes. She's tired from working all day and doesn't want to do the dishes right away. Her husband is stressed from family obligations, and he doesn't have the energy to do the dishes himself.

One strategy they could take to solve the problem of who will wash the dishes is to allow their fatigue and frustration to rule their behavior and argue over who *should* do them. But that approach could turn ugly quickly, sparking more difficult feelings and behavior.

If the woman wants to approach the situation from an NVC perspective, she could begin with an unarguable fact: There are dirty dishes in the sink, and neither she nor her husband wants to wash them. She might think it's unfair that he expects her to wash them, and he might have similar thoughts about her. Normally, they would argue about this. But tonight, she has a moment of insight. She realizes that they're caught in the same loop again and that their interpretations of the situation (e.g., that it's unfair of him to expect her to wash them, and vice versa) are not objective truths.

Seeking both a connection with her husband and a quick resolution to the dishes situation, she pauses for a second. She recognizes that she's just tired and cranky from a long day, and her husband is also exhausted. She reminds herself that it's important to both of them to have a clean home. Maybe her husband wouldn't mind too much if she did the dishes first thing in the morning. She acknowledges that both of them are tired and asks if he would mind if she did the dishes first thing the following day. He nods in agreement, and they snuggle on the couch to watch some TV.

NVC is not a surefire way to avoid arguments, but it can be an effective strategy to defuse them and reach mutually agreeable conclusions. The point is that it's often more efficient and fulfilling to first reach a connection regarding feelings and needs before pursuing a solution. Often, simply feeling seen by the other person—or by yourself—is sufficient, and you find yourself content, even if your original ask is not met.

Further Reading

1. "How to Create Win-Win Situations Using NVC": https://youtube.com/watch?v=V-UIj01jZBE.

2. "NVC Marshall Rosenberg - San Francisco Workshop": https://youtube.com/watch?v=l7TONauJGfc.

3. The Center for Nonviolent Communication: https://cnvc.org/.

Tool 2.2:
Prefer Requests over Demands

Be aware of your demands and, when appropriate, convert them into requests.

Motivation

When we ask other people to do something, we often come with a demanding energy, which sends a message that the other person must do as we ask—or else. This can happen even when the language we use seemingly contains only a request. For a request to be pure, we must be willing to accept a refusal. When we make hidden demands, the person who hears them may sense that there will be negative repercussions unless they agree.

This may create an awkward or even hostile atmosphere. Most people tend to rebel against demands and prefer to make free choices. Even if they agree to a request, they may not do so willingly. As a result, they may develop a sense of resentment, which may come back to hurt you or the relationship.

In situations where you feel compelled to make a demand but want to transform it into a request, you should process your emotions before communicating it. This can lead to a softer approach, which will probably be better received.

Benefits

- By allowing others to say "no," you can trust that when they say "yes," they mean it.
- If you do make a demand, being explicit can be quite effective.
- Receiving a request feels more pleasant than receiving a demand.

Challenges

- Allowing the possibility of refusal is often scary, painful, and difficult.
- Converting demands to requests can take a lot of time, energy, and attention.

Application

Before converting requests to demands, the first step is becoming aware of circumstances in which you tend to make demands. Sometimes, these can be easy to identify (e.g., when your language or tone is clearly demanding). At other times, distinguishing between requests and demands can be more subtle. A good rule of thumb is to imagine beforehand what would happen if the other party refused your requests. If you can see yourself responding with anger or withdrawal, there's a good chance you are about to make a demand, not a request. Genuine requests honor the other person's autonomy and right to decline.

If you realize that you're bringing a demanding energy, you now have a choice. You can proceed, which might be suitable in certain situations. As a parent, you may need to demand that your child stays off a dangerous road. As a branch manager at McDonald's, you demand that your employees work for the duration of their shift and dress in the company uniform. Cases where your boundaries are threatened might also be good candidates for demands. In general, however, you will probably find that leaving room for creativity and personal expression leads to better relationships with your kids, your employees, and people overall.

In case you decide you want to do the internal work of distilling a request out of a demand, here's a deeper form of the exercise above. Take some time for yourself and imagine a prospective encounter. Visualize yourself stating what you want and need and imagine the potential responses. Start by envisioning a "yes" and sit with how that feels inside your body. This should be a warm, pleasant feeling, which connects you to the reason you're making this request.

Next, imagine what might happen if you get a "no." Again, feel whatever emotions this stirs in you. Give yourself room to experience whatever needs aren't met by the other person's refusal and try to empathize with their needs as well. Understanding the reasons behind their potential refusal can help you accept it, and mourning what you won't receive in this scenario is key to truly accepting it. This can involve grieving how the specific ways you want your needs to be met don't work for the other person. Sometimes, it may include grieving the fact that some of your needs will only be met partially, or not at all, either in the moment or over a longer period of time.

Agreeing to feel the pain of the world not being the way you want it to be has a curative aspect. If you do it deeply, it can be a key to accepting whatever exists, including the other person's lack of will or ability to oblige your requests.

Tool 2.3:
Use a Talking Stick

Pick an object and decide that only its holder can speak.

Motivation

When you find yourself in an environment where people are frequently interrupting each other, this tool can help to eliminate (or at least drastically reduce) interruptions, increasing the quality and depth of the conversation.

Benefits

- Helps keep discourse peaceful and free of interruptions.
- Everyone feels heard and respected.
- There's more space to express complex or difficult topics.

Challenges

- Everybody must agree to abide by this method, which can sometimes be tricky.
- When you have something really pressing to say, you may find it hard to pay attention to others.

Application

This tool can be useful in a broad range of settings, from work meetings to personal conversations to the family dinner table. It's valuable in both personal and formal settings; you may want to explore it simply when you want to hold a sharing session with a partner or friends. Mediating exchanges with a talking stick can be an excellent way to foster intimacy.

First, it's crucial that everyone in your group agrees to use this technique, as it is only effective when people are on board with it. When everyone in the group consents, choose an object that will become the speaking object for the duration of your conversation. Traditionally, people often use a stick as the object, but for practical purposes, it can be anything small enough to hold but large enough for others to easily see.

The agreement in a talking stick circle is that the only person who can speak is the person holding the object. When one person has taken their turn, they put the object down somewhere everyone else can reach it or pass it to someone else who has indicated that they would like to speak. The object should never be grabbed by force, only picked up or given voluntarily. This technique gives everyone a chance to express themselves and have the opportunity to be fully heard. The other participants might want to keep a paper and pen ready to note down any thoughts they would like to share when it's their turn to hold the stick.

For this tool to be effective, it relies on all participants respecting one another and, for example, not keeping hold of the talking stick for an unreasonable length of time. Whenever you're holding the talking stick, you have a responsibility not to abuse your privilege.

On the other hand, if you want to speak, you can request that the holder pass the talking stick to you, although they are not obligated to respect your wishes. Using a talking stick can reveal conversational dynamics that previously went unremarked, such as one person holding the floor for an excessive period or another feeling too shy to take their turn. At its best, this tool can be a way to heal those dynamics and ensure that everyone gets a chance to contribute to the conversation.

Further Reading

The Speaker-Listener Technique: https://3.nd.edu/~pmtrc/Handouts/Speaker_Listener_with_Example.pdf.

Tool 2.4:
Postmortem After Arguments

Following a disagreement, independently evaluate what you personally could have done differently.

Motivation

After an argument, there is a natural tendency to forget about it and try to go back to normal. If this is done too quickly—without taking the time to learn and grow—the same issues may resurface at a later time. This tool can facilitate each person taking responsibility for their actions while also seeing their partner acknowledging their part in the conflict.

Benefits

- Changing yourself is often more productive than trying to change your partner.
- Knowing that you and your partner are both committed to this process can bring you closer.

Challenges

- Sometimes, you may not find anything in your behavior you want to change.
- It can be hard to move past judging or competing with the other person and focus on learning from what happened.

Application

This tool is something Jordan Peterson suggests in his book *12 Rules for Life* (see Tool 3.10: Twelve Rules for Life). After arguing with someone, split up and go to different rooms to think of at least one small thing you could have done differently in the events leading up to the fight or can do better in the future. Each of you should focus on changing your own actions: what *you* personally could have done differently. Be as honest as possible with yourself and try to expand your thinking rather than getting stuck in your usual patterns.

This process can take just a minute or two—or considerably longer. You may find several aspects of your behavior that you wish to change or just one small thing like, "I wish I had paused for three seconds before replying to you." However long this process takes, when both of you have determined something you want to change, meet up again and share what you came up with. At times, it may be difficult to find something you want to change, but if you look hard enough, there's always something.

The point of this tool is not to try to change the other person or prove that you're right, but rather to investigate what you could do better, learn from it, and improve. If you can forego blame after an argument and instead take the opportunity to grow both as individuals and together, you may discover ways in which you truly want to change. This can be a very powerful way of sharing a journey with your partner and strengthening the relationship.

Further Reading

Jordan Peterson, *12 Rules for Life: An Antidote for Chaos* (Random House, Canada, 2018).

Tool 2.5:
Mega Threads

When addressing sensitive issues,
try intensive asynchronous correspondence.

Motivation

Suppose you have complex issues with another person that you can't seem to resolve in the usual ways. You've tried talking about them and maybe explored therapy, but the issues remain frustratingly persistent. Whenever you communicate about this, one or both of you gets triggered and stops listening to the other person. In these situations, it might be helpful to take a step back and try switching to a slower medium of communication. Mega Threads—long threads of online communication—can be one such medium.

Utilizing Mega Threads will allow each of you to process your issues in your own time, when you have sufficient resources and are not emotionally triggered. With this technique, there's almost no limit to the depth of your response to a particular issue, so you have quite a lot of room to express yourself fully and to be heard.

Benefits

- You can choose a good time to work on sensitive issues, ensuring you are calm and in the right state of mind.

- You can express yourself fully, without the other person interrupting you.

- Each person can write at their own pace and time, bridging gaps in communication styles between partners.

- You can process your triggers on your own time instead of reacting automatically and lashing out.

Challenges

- Corresponding about emotional issues can feel difficult or disconnected for some people.
- Fully expressing yourself in this format can be very time- and energy-consuming.
- Slight ambiguities in phrasing can lead to radical misinterpretations.

Application

To begin, get your partner's agreement to try out this tool—not everyone likes to communicate using huge chunks of text! If they are willing to try it out, establish a common communication channel. Note: This should not be a channel you are already using for other purposes because, as the name suggests, Mega Threads can be quite large and intensive. You don't want the Mega Thread clogging up your other text communications. It's better to open a dedicated group for the two of you on WhatsApp or iMessage, start an email thread, or create a shared Google Doc. Find whatever method works best for you.

To begin, create the Mega Thread by picking one or more topics you want to work on. Take a big breath and start writing about the situation at hand, expressing everything that's on your mind: all your feelings, needs, wants, desires, fears, grudges, and blames. For this to be most effective, it's best to include trigger warnings above any text that might be particularly difficult for your partner to read and/or add statements of love and goodwill. Prefacing especially sensitive sentiments with a disclaimer or reminding your partner that you care can help you be fully heard. At these points, you can ask them to stop reading and breathe before proceeding or explain that you're describing your inner thoughts and voices, which might include parts of yourself that you're not wholly identified with. This can help them get into a more receptive state and allow them to read your words without overreacting.

After you've fully expressed yourself, it's your partner's turn. It's important for them to pick a good time to reply, while they are present and relatively calm and have ample time. They then respond to everything you wrote in a similar manner, explaining their side of the issues. Either after they finish replying to everything or perhaps before they reply, they can add new topics that bother them.

This type of discussion can have a tendency to branch out into other side topics, quickly developing into an extremely large, unwieldy thread. To manage this tendency, it's helpful to identify tricky side topics and file them separately in a backlog, perhaps in Excel or Google Sheets, for later processing. This ensures that the main thread doesn't become too big to handle and simultaneously prevents you from forgetting anything important. After the main thread has subsided, you can pick new topics to process from the backlog.

You can employ Mega Threads in a focused effort to address one specific subject or as an ongoing tool to process issues as they arise. After going back and forth a few times on a topic, hopefully you'll feel at least some relief and mutual understanding.

Tool 2.6:
Active Listening

Listen with full intent instead of waiting to speak.

Motivation

Often, when people engage in discourse, they unintentionally default to focusing on their own thoughts. Instead of listening, they spend their time waiting for the other person to stop speaking so they can say what's on their mind. As a result, they don't pay full attention to what is being said and don't internalize the speaker's message or fully connect on an emotional level. Even worse, they may respond in a way that makes it clear they have not been listening, which may irritate the speaker and make them feel unheard.

This style of conversation leads easily to miscommunication, conflict, and feelings of underappreciation. Active listening is a useful approach when you want to create respectful conversations in which you fully understand what is being said. It often leads to improved communication, fewer disagreements, and feelings of appreciation.

Benefits

- Having a better understanding of what people say to you.
- Other people feel heard and understood.

Challenges

- It can be hard to resist planning your reply instead of being fully present during a conversation.
- Sometimes, random thoughts can grab you while you're trying to listen.

Application

When practicing active listening, you consciously maintain focus on hearing what the other person is saying. One way to do this is to silently repeat their words in your mind. If you notice your mind wandering, you can quickly bring your attention back to listening.

If you sense that your partner might feel misunderstood, you may want to try another step. When your conversation partner is done talking, paraphrase what they have said and repeat it back to them instead of replying right away. This is to assure them that you understand. Then, you can check in with them to be sure you understand correctly and fully. The other person may want to clarify things, correct you, or add some more details. Let them. Then you can offer your response.

When you're listening to someone and possible replies or questions occur to you, you may want to note them down on a piece of paper so they don't distract you while you are listening. At first, your conversation partner might not understand why you're taking notes and feel uncomfortable. To reassure them, it's a good idea to communicate ahead of the conversation that you may take notes in order to listen better.

Tool 2.7:
Radical Honesty

Tell the truth, or at least don't lie.[5]

Motivation

When you want to live freely, openly, and at ease, without tension created by maintaining falsehoods, radical honesty is your answer. Most people lie every now and then without giving it much thought. Sometimes, these lies are harmless. But more often than not, they come with costs that can be hard to anticipate. When lying is a habit, covering up for lies with more lies also becomes a habit, and managing this web takes enormous emotional and cognitive effort. The alternative is making a conscious effort to tell the truth, or at least not to lie. While scary at first, over time this can greatly simplify your communications and increase trust.

Benefits

- Simplifies our communication and frees us from the tension created by lying and covering up for lies.
- Creates deeper connections with people and facilitates more sustainable relationships.
- Choosing to tell the truth makes you trustworthy and enables you to trust others more easily.

Challenges

- Complicated situations are sometimes difficult to talk about openly.

---

[5] The term "radical honesty" was coined in a book of the same name by Brad Blanton. This phrasing doesn't come directly from the book, but instead it is Rule 8 in Jordan Peterson's book *12 Rules for Life* (see Tool 3.10: Twelve Rules for Life).

- Truth can hurt people and may push them away. To sustain honesty while minimizing pain and fostering connection takes skill and compassion.
- Balancing privacy with a commitment to the truth can be tricky.

Application

Radical honesty is not about sharing everything on your mind. It is simply about being completely honest and refraining from lying—even from telling little white lies or making inaccurate statements. Honesty can sometimes be inconvenient or even dangerous. In situations when you are tempted to bend the truth a bit, trust that, in the long term, choosing to be truthful will be worth it. Of course, in an extreme case where there's a risk of physical danger to you or others, lying might still be a valid option.

It takes skill to tell the truth in a way that safeguards you and others. You might want to assess whether the other person wants to hear your truth and whether the current setting is appropriate. Try to anticipate how what you need to say will affect them emotionally and adjust your delivery accordingly. You can also ask the other person in advance: "Can I be completely honest here? Is this a good time?"

A commitment to honesty doesn't mean you must share everything on your mind with everybody. Helpful phrases to lean on when you don't feel comfortable speaking the truth can be, "I don't want to answer that question," or "That's private."

Further Reading

1. Brad Blanton, *Radical Honesty: How to Transform Your Life by Telling the Truth* (Sparrowhawk Publications, 2005).
2. Jordan Peterson, *12 Rules for Life: An Antidote to Chaos* (Random House, 2018).

Tool 2.8:
When Triggered, Pause

If you're struggling to regulate your emotions, take a break.

Motivation

Sometimes conversations touch on sensitive topics, leading one or more participants to become emotionally triggered. In this state, people experience diminished self-control and may default to survival-oriented behavioral patterns, making it difficult for them to communicate effectively. Instead of being present and responding to what's happening in the here and now, they may enter a fight/flight/freeze mode where they are reacting to past trauma.

When you recognize that you or someone you're talking to may be triggered, it can be helpful to take a pause and allow that person's nervous system an opportunity to calm down and reorganize.

Benefits

- Nonreactive conversations have a connected quality, unlike most habitual communication.
- Even a brief pause can be enough to turn a conversation around.
- It takes two to argue but only one to de-escalate.

Challenges

- Noticing that you're triggered can be hard, especially in a real-time conversation when you're also listening and responding to another person.
- In a heated moment, telling another person that you think they're triggered can inflame the situation further.
- Your decision to take a break might not be well received.

Application

When you find your emotions getting the best of you during a conversation, that may be a sign to pause. In order to reconnect with yourself, you can take a couple of breaths or ask for a few minutes apart. To reassure the other person, you can tell them that you're not abandoning the difficult topic; you're just taking care of yourself so you can process it better and be more present with them. It's best not to check your phone or otherwise distract yourself but instead use the time to tune in to your body and breathing.

If you're low on emotional resources, a few minutes' break might be insufficient; you may need hours or days to process. Ideally, stating your need for a break should be done skillfully and effectively, which may take practice. Take care of yourself and ask for what you need—hopefully, your partner will understand. Even if they don't, your needs are your responsibility. Nobody can force you to be in a conversation you're not ready for.

An alternative to taking a break is slowing down and keeping the conversation going while staying present. If you want, you may also ask the other person to slow down, preferably in a way that respects their freedom to refuse (see Tool 2.2: Prefer Requests over Demands).

A good indication that you are ready to continue is that you can empathize with the other person. This doesn't mean you need to agree with them—only that you're able to see things from their point of view while simultaneously maintaining your own. If you come to the interaction with empathy, odds are you'll connect better and be more likely to realize your goals in the conversation and relationship.

Being triggered in a conversation isn't necessarily a sign that something is wrong. Difficult conversations are a part of all meaningful relationships. This tool is about creating the space to conduct them effectively while also protecting your boundaries and keeping everyone involved safe.

Further Reading

1. Kerry Lusignan, "Love Smart by Learning When to Take a Break," The Gottman Institute, last updated June 25, 2024, https://gottman.com/blog/love-smarter-learning-take-break/.

2. Emma Todd Carpenter, "Stonewalling and Taking a Break Are Not the Same Thing," *Family Perspectives* 2, no.1, article 10 (2020), https://scholarsarchive.byu.edu/familyperspectives/vol2/iss1/10/.

Tool 2.9:
Forgiveness

Free yourself from the burden of anger and resentment.

Motivation

The quote that opens this chapter sums up the value of forgiveness: "If we could read the secret history of our enemies, we should find in each man's life sorrow and suffering enough to disarm our hostility."

The implication here is that forgiveness is something we do not do for those who have wronged us but for ourselves. When we forgive others, we free ourselves from the weight of resentment and anger. Refusing to forgive others maintains those painful emotions, stoking the fires of bitterness.

This is especially true in ongoing relationships. It's one thing to forgive a hurt in a long-dormant connection and move on. It's another to forgive someone you see regularly. In this case, an inability to forgive can prevent the relationship from attaining its true potential, affecting future behavior on both sides.

Benefits

- The ability to let go of emotional charges that burden you brings relief and inner peace.

- Anger blocks the flow of energy, which can eventually come back to haunt you. Releasing it frees you from this cycle.

Challenges

- Forgiving people without protecting yourself can open you up to further harm.

- Sometimes, the price of forgiving a painful wound can be too high.

Application

In the first book of his renowned *Conversations with God* series (see Tool 6.10: Conversations with God), Neale Donald Walsch discusses forgiveness and how to go about it at length. He describes a road to forgiveness that embraces the worldview that we're all one—we're all the same. We are all parts of God, trying to meet our needs, and we all have triggers and histories of trauma, which can prompt us to behave in inappropriate ways. This may sound like a cliché, but when we tap into this idea of forgiveness, we can focus our energy on realizing that people are caught up in their own lives and trying to meet their own universal needs (see Tool 2.1: Nonviolent Communication). Having a little empathy can go a long way!

Forgiving others requires us to value them as human beings and acknowledge that they are damaged and hurt in some way. The idea that to know someone is to love them points to this path of forgiveness. When we truly understand others, we see that people behave meanly when they themselves are hurting. Functional people do not intentionally engage in dysfunctional behavior.

Accessing forgiveness is not easy, but one method is to reflect on the reasons for another's poor behavior. If someone hurts you, try thinking about why they might be acting out—which needs of theirs are not being met. If you're able to understand what is lacking in their lives, you may be able to feel compassion for their pain and, from there, forgive them.

Importantly, however, this doesn't mean allowing them to continue hurting you. Forgiveness and enabling are quite different. It's admirable to strive to forgive others, but where necessary, it's important to maintain personal boundaries and protect yourself from continuing harm. Forgiveness and boundaries can exist simultaneously, and it's up to you to maintain the balance of the two.

Further Reading

1. Neale Donald Walsch, *Conversations with God: An Uncommon Dialogue* (Hodder and Stouton, 1977).

2. Tara Brach, "Free Yourself from Blame & Resentment," Insight-Timer, https://insighttimer.com/meditation-courses/course_free-yourself-from-blame-and-resentment.

Tool 2.10:
Silence

Sometimes, it's useful to let awkward silences happen.

Motivation

When a break occurs in conversation, it's common for people to try to fill the empty space by speaking, even when they don't have anything particular to say. For example, let's say someone has asked a question and the other person hasn't answered right away. It's common for the asker to jump in and provide an answer themselves. In this scenario, however, if the asker can hold their tongue, the other person will have time to provide a fully formed, authentic response.

Another scenario in which this tool could be useful is during emotional conversations. You might get triggered and feel the need to answer right away. If you hold your tongue and take some time to process, you might find a response more aligned with your whole self.

Benefits

- People have the time to fully express themselves.
- Removes pressure to artificially fill the conversational void.
- Leaves room for people to think and feel.

Challenges

- People often feel responsible for keeping the conversation alive.

Application

Learn to be quiet until there's an authentic need to speak. This requires being in touch with yourself and identifying whether your reason for talking serves you at that moment. If you feel uncomfortable with the silence and notice thoughts such as "It's my turn to say something—it will be weird if I don't" or "I'm boring the other person," that's a good sign that your desire to speak might not be serving a deeper need. If your reason to talk comes from an intention to deepen the conversation or share something personal, that's a good cue to share.

Tool 2.11:
Respect Others' Autonomy When Offering Advice

When sharing guidance, do it freely without strings attached.

Motivation

When you think you know what's best for another person or what the right course of action is for them, it is natural to wish to offer advice. If you become attached to the idea that others should follow your advice, however, you are setting yourself up for heartache and grievance, which can really harm your relationship with them.

On the other hand, if you can give advice generously and accept that others will do as they see fit, you can rest easy knowing that you have offered guidance, whether or not they choose to act on it. This protects your relationship and also leaves the door open for them to choose whether and when to apply your counsel.

Benefits

- Frees you from the stress and struggle of feeling that others are not fulfilling your expectations.
- Allows others the freedom to make up their minds.

Challenges

- It's hard to be truly unattached. Even if you don't express expectations, you may hold on to them internally, and others will likely feel this.

Application

There are times when we become aware that someone is embracing ideas or engaging in activities that we don't believe are best for them.

They might invite us to offer advice on and insight into their situation. Or we may catch ourselves thinking that we know the optimal course of action and wishing to offer them advice that we hope will prove helpful.

Before acting on this impulse, it is wise to ask ourselves why we feel compelled to tell others what to do? Are we trying to control their behavior? Are we attached to a specific outcome? If the answer to these last two questions is yes, it may be beneficial to refrain from saying anything. Otherwise, there is a risk that you will put pressure both on yourself and on them, potentially straining your relationship.

It may be helpful to remind yourself that others have the right to live their lives, just as you have the right to live yours. If you feel you must provide advice, it can be helpful to draw on your own personal experience and background, sharing what you have learned, as opposed to simply telling them they are wrong and should behave differently.

Another thing you can try before speaking is to imagine offering your best advice and having it rejected out of hand. If the person you advised did the complete opposite of what you suggested, would that trigger an emotional response in you? If so, taking a moment to consciously acknowledge and feel these emotions can defuse a lot of the potential sting later on.

Tool 2.12:
Wheel of Consent

A framework for investigating and playing with relationship roles, created by Betty Martin.

Motivation

Sometimes, we may feel that our relationships are becoming stagnant. We may simply wish to better understand our interpersonal dynamics, or we may want to try out new roles, experiencing ourselves in new ways. The Wheel of Consent, a concept originally created by Betty Martin, is a tool to support this process within appropriate boundaries and structure. It highlights the four roles we can take on in relationships and, by bringing them to conscious awareness, invites us to experiment with them. It is usually applied in a sexual context, although the principles are relevant to all aspects of communication.

Most of us naturally gravitate to one of the four roles that make up the Wheel of Consent. Once we become aware of our favored role, we can consciously decide to explore others, expanding our minds and challenging our own and others' preconceptions. This can be very exciting and fulfilling.

Benefits

- You can use the wheel to analyze elements of your relationship and guide you to where you might want to be.
- Having a framework for understanding and guiding your explorations can bring you safety and reassurance.

Challenges

- You might have preconceptions about some of these roles, which can limit your capacity to explore them openly.

- Each role has its shadow side. Therefore, it's vital to get informed consent from your partner to ensure that you stay on the light side and are both safe.

Application

The Wheel of Consent contains four distinct positions that people can adopt within a relationship. These are:

- Taker
- Allower
- Giver
- Receiver

For the Wheel of Consent to function effectively, each person must agree to the implications of each role. The Taker consents to take from the Allower, and the Allower consents to having the Taker take. The Giver consents to give to the Receiver, who in turn consents to receive from the Giver.

Martin invented a three-minute game inviting participants to intentionally spend three minutes in each quadrant, exploring the potential of the different roles. For example, the Taker could say to her partner, "I want to touch you." If the Allower agrees to this request, he nods his consent and allows the Taker to touch him however she wants for three minutes without touching her back. Then, they switch roles for three minutes: The Taker becomes the Allower, and vice versa, and the new Taker makes a request according to his desires. Participants can also make more specific requests, such as "I want to touch you anywhere above the waist." In this case, the Allower might agree to the entire request or modify it by saying something like "I agree to you touching me, but only above the shoulders."

To complete the Wheel of Consent, each partner experiences each role for three minutes, so the game proceeds with both taking on the mantle of Giver and Receiver. Partners take time to investigate the

THE WHEEL OF CONSENT

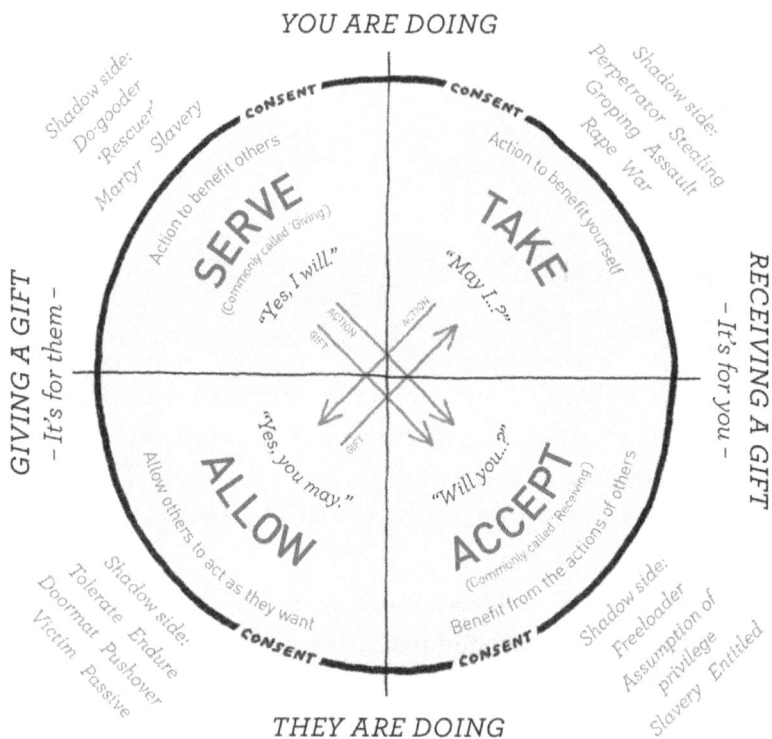

YOU ARE DOING

Shadow side:
Do-gooder
'Rescuer'
Martyr   Slavery

CONSENT

Action to benefit others

SERVE
(Commonly called 'Giving')
"Yes, I will."

CONSENT

Shadow side:
Perpetrator   Stealing
Groping   Assault
Rape   War

Action to benefit yourself

TAKE
"May I...?"

GIVING A GIFT
– It's for them –

ACTION
GIFT

ACTION
GIFT

RECEIVING A GIFT
– It's for you –

"Yes, you may."

ALLOW
Allow others to act as they want

"Will you...?"

ACCEPT
(Commonly called 'Receiving')

Benefit from the actions of others

Shadow side:
Tolerate   Endure
Doormat   Pushover
Victim   Passive

CONSENT

Shadow side:
Freeloader
Assumption of
privilege
Slavery   Entitled

CONSENT

THEY ARE DOING

In any instance of touch, there are two factors: who is doing and who it's for. Those two factors combine in four ways (quadrants). Each quadrant presents its own challenges, lessons and joys.

The circle represents consent (your agreement). Inside the circle there is a gift given and a gift received. Outside the circle (without consent) the same action becomes stealing, abusing, etc.

© Dr. Betty Martin / www.bettymartin.org
You are welcome to share, including this diagram, with attribution (leave this paragraph in).

boundaries of each role, exploring their habits and desires. In healthy relationships, both people consent to their roles and respect their own and each other's boundaries, experimenting with new roles to determine whether something else feels better. If you are used to playing the Giver, you may enjoy becoming the Receiver. If you usually slip into the role of the Allower, it may be a thrill to be the Taker for a while.

You should be aware of the shadow sides of each role. The Receiver's shadow side is the freeloader, who assumes privilege and entitlement. The shadow of the Taker is the thief or perpetrator. The Allower's shadow is tolerating mistreatment, while the Giver's shadow is the rescuer, the do-gooder who invades others' space. It's valuable to experiment with different roles, but it's important not to allow shadow sides to dominate, as these can cause rifts and toxicity in relationships.

Further Reading

Videos on the Wheel of Consent: https://bettymartin.org/videos/.

Tool 2.13:
Make and Formalize Agreements

Keep track of your written and oral agreements with yourself and others.

Motivation

In daily life, we frequently make ambiguous or unspoken agreements, which we then interpret based on our individual memory and understanding. This understanding may or may not match the perception of other parties. Without a formal record, this may lead to frustration and conflict as two (or more) people have a different understanding of what has been discussed. One solution is to record your agreements, preventing future grievances and arguments.

Not every agreement involves other people. Making agreements with yourself is a way to guide your behavior in specific situations. For example, let's say you agree—for yourself—only to eat ice cream once a week. When you're at the ice cream shop and tempted to order a cone, your agreement will act like an inner parent, anchoring you and assisting you in making the choice your higher self would make.

Benefits

- Formalizing agreements provides all parties with a clear understanding of expectations, reducing the likelihood of misunderstandings.
- Proactively prevents future grievances and arguments, which fosters smoother interactions and relationships.
- Agreements, even with oneself, act as a valuable behavioral framework, encouraging self-discipline and intentional decision-making.

Challenges

- Some people may perceive formalizing agreements as unnecessary or cumbersome.

- Ensuring total consistency and preventing differing interpretations can be challenging, potentially leading to long and tedious agreements.

Application

The first step to formalizing agreements is to ask for the consent of everyone involved. An agreement won't hold if anyone feels that they didn't enter into it willingly. Some people find the idea of entering into formal agreements in a relationship context off-putting. They may feel constrained or perceive it as work. If this is the case, be sure to take the preferences of others into account. Don't be so blinded by enthusiasm for this tool that you railroad others into participation. Once everyone is comfortable, the next step is to negotiate the terms of the agreement. Who will do what? When? In what circumstances?

It's important, too, to check that everyone understands the agreement to mean the same thing. If there's ambiguity, that can lead to differing interpretations and potential conflict further down the line. Once you have a clear agreement in place, document it using whatever method works best for you. This can be pen and paper, a note on your phone, or anything else you prefer. For easy reference, maintain a centralized record in a shared document or folder. Keep your agreements as concise as possible while ensuring they cover relevant circumstances.

To make your agreements airtight, consider including specific terms, such as time frames or other conditions, that might affect their validity. One way to do this is to pursue SMART (Specific, Measurable, Achievable, Relevant, and Time-Bound) goals. Constructing your agreement using this framework can help you ensure that your agreement is robust. That said, try not to be *too* rigid. Creating an agreement shouldn't feel like a torturous experience—hopefully, it can even be fun.

To give you an idea of how this might work, here's an example of an agreement in practice:

> "I can cancel our meetings up to forty-eight hours in advance with no penalty. If I cancel with less than forty-eight hours' notice, I will pay for the session."

This is clear and concise and meets the SMART criteria.

In challenging situations, you could agree to disagree for a while and perhaps generate a set time frame for revisiting the topic in the hopes that you will be able to reach a more complete settlement at a later date.

You can also renegotiate agreements as circumstances or relationships evolve. Some people fear that if they agree to something, then they will be bound to it on a permanent basis. For these people, knowing they will have a chance to renegotiate can be an enormous relief. It may even be the difference between engaging with this process and resisting it. Others may respond with anxiety because they like the certainty of knowing where they stand. To make this tool successful, you'll need to be aware of your own and the other parties' personalities and craft the agreement accordingly.

Finally, know that this tool isn't limited to interactions with others; it's just as powerful for personal development. Whenever you want a formalized framework to guide your behavior or support your progress toward personal goals, you can craft agreements with yourself. And, just as you do with others, you can agree to disagree for a while, come back to them later, or renegotiate agreements that no longer work for you.

Further Reading

1. Kimberlee Leonard and Rob Watts, "The Ultimate Guide to S.M.A.R.T. Goals," *Forbes* Advisor, last updated July 9, 2024, https://forbes.com/advisor/business/smart-goals/.

2. Cami McLaren, "Keeping Agreements with Yourself," McLaren Coaching, https://mclarencoaching.com/keeping-agreements-with-yourself/.

3. Andee Tagle and Clare Marie Schneider, "From Housework to Sex, Here's How Relationship Contracts Can Help Couples," NPR, last updated December 21, 2022, https://npr.org/2021/08/01/1022875293/relationship-contracts-couples-useful-advice-tips.

Tool 2.14:
Personal Operating Manual

A way to record the key values and preferences of those who matter to you.

Motivation

When you are close to someone and love them, you may wish to actively find ways to increase their happiness, understand their values, or otherwise enrich their life. However, it can be hard to remember all the key details about others, even those whom you care about deeply.

One way to solve this problem is by creating a personal operating manual for them. Whenever you learn something new about them, noting it serves as a reminder of what they like and don't like, enabling you to retain this information and behave accordingly.

Benefits

- Helps you learn the best ways to communicate with significant people in your life.
- Can include a repository of things they enjoy, making it easier for you to express your love and affection in ways they appreciate.

Challenges

- Some people may find the concept too clinical and fear that it replaces a more heartfelt understanding.

Application

Ideally, begin by approaching the person you want to create a personal operating manual for and mentioning that you would like to explore this idea. Technically, you do not need their permission before creating this type of manual, but it's nicer to do this with consent. Reassure them that they don't need to do anything; you will do all the work, and they will benefit from your increased understanding of them.

The execution is relatively straightforward. Whenever you learn something new about your partner, make a note of it, either in a handwritten journal or an online document. Every argument, humorous exchange, or gentle discourse holds clues to deciphering their personality.

Your personal operating manual should serve as a live document where you note favorite foods, reactions to gifts, and other preferences. If you approach them when they're angry, what facilitates smooth conversation and what doesn't? What are their moods and principles? You can even ask deep questions such as "What is your purpose in life?" or "What's your biggest regret?" and record the answers.

The key to making your personal operating manual usable is periodically reviewing and organizing the information you collect so that when you want to retrieve it, you know how to find what you're looking for. When you do this, you can peruse it at any time and reflect on what you're learning. This process will help you discover what truly motivates the other person, what turns them on, what intrigues them, what they dislike, and more.

Tool 2.15:
Acknowledge When You're Triggered

When you are feeling emotionally unstable
or overwhelmed, own it.

Motivation

When any person in a conversation is angry, scared, or defensive, it's extremely difficult to communicate productively. No doubt you've experienced such situations in which you've struggled to control your thoughts and think clearly.

This happens to everyone. When you find yourself overreacting or feeling overwhelmed, it can be helpful to openly acknowledge your emotional state. This gives you a chance to breathe, calm down, and be seen.

Benefits

- Helps prevent arguments from escalating.
- Nurtures trust between you and others.

Challenges

- In the heat of the moment, both recognizing and naming your heightened emotional state can be very difficult.

Application

In order for this tool to be useful, you must be able to notice and honor your emotions in real time. Therefore, it is more about your relationship with yourself than with others.

When you notice an interaction approaching a boiling point to the extent that your defensiveness, anxiety, or other strong emotions are beginning to overrule your rational mind, simply accept and acknowledge what's happening. As clearly and nonjudgmentally as you can, inform the other person that you are triggered (see Tool 2.7: Radical Honesty). Take a moment to think about what you need right now. Do you need a quick break? Would you like to continue the conversation a bit more slowly? Whatever it is, ask for it.

If your conversational partner is in a relatively calm state, they may be able to empathize. In this case, they may seek to understand what's happening and help you. If they, too, are on the verge of being triggered, however, it might be best for you to separate until you both feel more at ease.

Given how challenging it can be to recognize and name your emotions in the moment, especially when that moment is highly charged, you may find it valuable to memorize a few phrases you can draw on at these times. For example:

- I'm not in the right emotional place to have this conversation right now.
- I'm in control right now, but in ten seconds, I might not be.
- I'm feeling triggered and need a break.

Tool 2.16:
Talk About What's Happening Now

Use the present moment to deepen conversations.

Motivation

We all have surface conversations with certain people. We may feel comfortable discussing relatively inconsequential topics, such as the weather, sports, or work, but we fail to take the interaction into deeper, more meaningful territory.

If we continue to relate only on this level, we will never acquire a true understanding of these people or forge a closer relationship. In some cases, this may be acceptable—cordiality may be sufficient for us. Should we wish to connect more deeply, however, a great way to do so is by tapping into what's alive in us at a given moment and using it to guide the conversation to a deeper place.

Benefits

- Livens up conversations with fresh energy.
- Forges deeper, more meaningful connections.
- Can clear the air of unspoken tension, contributing to a healthier relationship.

Challenges

- Shifting a conversation in real time requires a high degree of emotional and situational awareness.
- Touching on deeper subjects can feel very uncomfortable or even scary.

Application

Deeper talks are a necessary component of discussing more important topics. Indeed, therapy works on this concept. When you see a therapist (see Chapter 3), you are expected not only to skim the surface of topics but also to dive deeper and discuss your true thoughts and emotions. In any context, one excellent way to cultivate depth is to focus on what feelings are alive in you right now.

Before you can talk about what you're experiencing in the present, you need to identify what it is that you're noticing. Perhaps your mind keeps slipping to a disturbing thought or emotion, or you're having trouble fully connecting to the conversation. One option is to ignore these feelings and make an effort to force yourself back to the existing interaction. Alternatively, you could choose to bring what's going on inside you to the surface of your awareness, then potentially into the conversation itself.

One occasion when you may find this conversational style especially useful is when you feel like there's an elephant in the room. A (metaphorical) elephant in the room is something large, unmissable, and important that, for one reason or another, is not being openly acknowledged. The fact that nobody's talking about it affects everybody and can cause numerous problems. Actively pointing out an undiscussed topic you see is a great way to bring it to conscious awareness and direct energy toward working on the issues it creates. This process won't necessarily be easy, but creating a shared reality is an essential first step.

At other times, you may be aware of something that's happening in your head and heart while the conversation moves around you. For example, a friend might be discussing a subject you have no interest in, and you can feel yourself starting to zone out. You might be curious about some aspect of a story but unsure whether to ask about it because you're worried it might embarrass someone—or simply lack tact. Maybe you're angry about something unrelated, and it's affecting your capacity to be present. Whatever the case, you can make a practice of beginning to notice your internal state and—when appropriate—giving voice to it.

Utilizing this tool doesn't mean you need to automatically share everything that's on your mind. Once you notice a thought or emotion, you have a choice: You can consider possible outcomes and make an informed decision (see Tool 1.10: Default to Openness).

Further Reading

1. Tool 2.6: Radical Honesty
2. Tool 2.1: Nonviolent Communication

Tool 2.17:
Ethical Nonmonogamy

There's more than one way to have a relationship.

Motivation

Some people wish for a broader range of life experiences, including a balance between commitment and variety in their relationships. Increasingly, many people find that they cannot imagine themselves committing to a monogamous relationship and living for fifty or sixty years with only one person. If this is your experience, you may find the concept of nonmonogamy helpful.

Nonmonogamy is based on the idea that it's possible to love and have relations with more than one person and that when we acknowledge this, we open ourselves up to new ways of living. It is not the same as cheating on your spouse or partner because in ethical nonmonogamy, every participant is aware of the situation and participates with full, informed consent.

Benefits

- The opportunity to experience more love, sexual relationships, and freedom.
- Doesn't put the weight of meeting all your needs on a single person.
- The complexity of navigating multiple relationships offers lots of opportunities for personal growth and self-development.

Challenges

- Opening an existing relationship requires consent, persistence, and a willingness to navigate the different needs of everyone involved. At times, this may prove impossible and lead to breakups.

- Due to the increased number of people involved in an open relationship structure, communication needs are exponentially greater.
- The intensity of both positive and negative emotions and the accompanying drama can be taxing.

Application

Although a nonmonogamous approach to relationships is becoming more common, many people still find the concept very challenging. Before taking any irreversible steps, such as telling your significant other you want to make the relationship polyamorous, do some research so that you understand the concept and its different expressions. There are several different styles of consensual nonmonogamy, such as swinging, open relationships, polyamory, and more, and it will be helpful if you understand which you find most appealing.

Your next step should be to discuss the idea with your existing partner, if you have one. Explain that you are interested in exploring an open relationship and be prepared to listen to their point of view. Try to be clear about your own desires and needs. Do you want to be sexually active with others, or do you wish to love more than one person and build those relationships simultaneously? Is opening up essential for you, or is it just a preference? Take into consideration that the very concept could be shocking to some people, and they might need time to process. To facilitate the conversation, you may wish to talk to a couple's therapist who is open to nonmonogamy (although not dogmatic about it).

Assuming your partner is willing (or if you are solo), you'll need to think about communication styles. Some people prefer a "don't ask, don't tell" approach to their partner's other connections, whereas others may prefer to know the people you're intimate with and perhaps

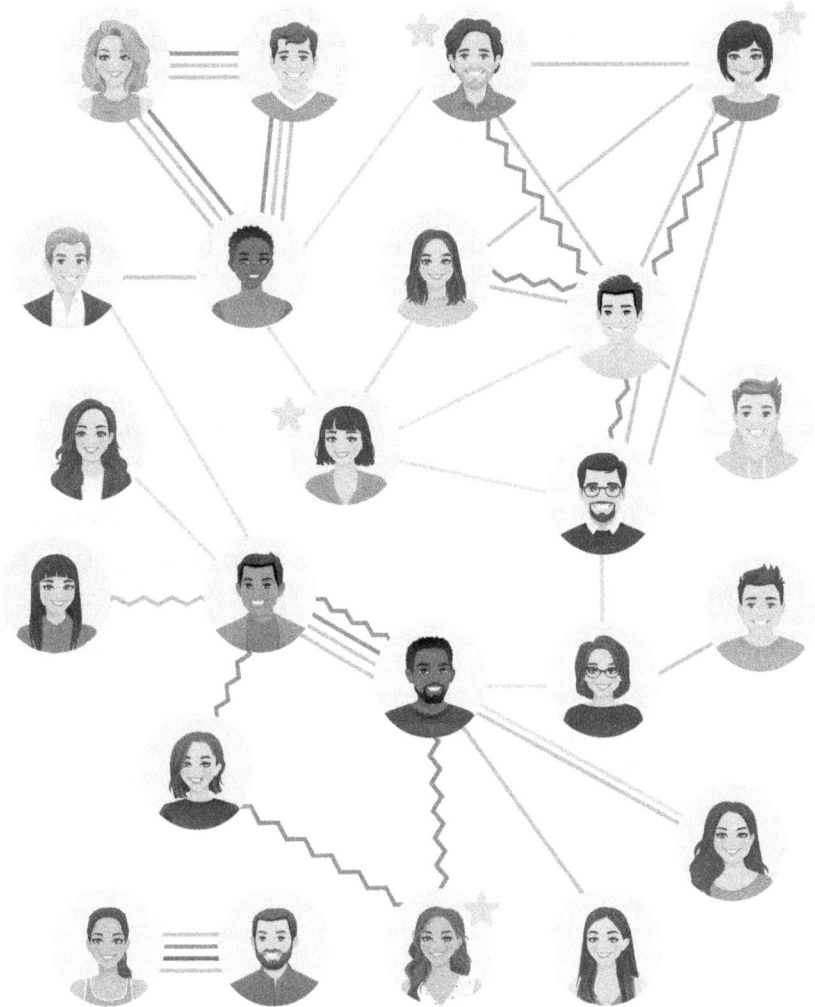

solo poly
co-parenting
cohabitating
sexual partnership
relationship anarchy

asexual / nonsexual partnership
long distance relationship
monogamous
mono-poly relationship
former partners

socialize together. It's essential that everyone is on the same page about the type of relationship structure they are agreeing to, but be aware that this structure can evolve over time.

A good next step could be finding an online or offline community of like-minded people. There are many safe, nonsexual spaces where people just meet and talk about nonmonogamy, many of which are friendly to newcomers. They can be a great place to hear different stories, learn about the good and bad, and assess whether a nonmonogamous lifestyle is for you. Ultimately, there are as many ways to do nonmonogamy as there are nonmonogamous people, and there are many resources to help you come to grips with it. While it can be an exciting and fulfilling way to live, it's also advisable to explore it thoroughly before doing anything irreversible.

Further Reading

1. Tristan Taormino, *Opening Up: A Guide to Creating and Sustaining Open Relationships* (Cleiss Press, 2008).

2. Dossie Easton and Janet W. Hardy, *The Ethical Slut, Third Edition: A Practical Guide to Polyamory, Open Relationships, and Other Freedoms in Sex and Love* (Ten Speed Press, 2017).

3. More Than Two, Franklin Veaux's polyamory site: https://morethantwo.com/.

4. Christopher Ryan and Cacilda Jethá, *Sex at Dawn: The Prehistoric Origins of Modern Sexuality* (HarperCollins, 2010).

Tool 2.18:
Express Your Emotions Numerically

Calibrate and communicate the intensity of your emotions.

Motivation

Expressing your emotions on a numeric scale—for example, from one to ten—can help you communicate your emotional state more accurately and give others useful information about how to interact with you. When others use this tool, you will understand them better and be able to assess an appropriate response.

Benefits

- Placing your emotions on a numerical scale can help you better understand yourself and your reactions.
- Communicating this scale to others can foster mutual understanding and create signposts in otherwise vague territory.

Challenges

- Not everyone interprets intensity the same way, so there may still be differences.
- Some people find describing their emotions in numbers uncomfortable.

Application

When you feel an intense emotion that you want to communicate with someone else, name the emotion and assign it a number from one to ten. For example, when you receive a gift that you really love, you may feel joy at an intensity of nine out of ten. When someone cuts you off on the road, you may feel frustration at an intensity of seven out of ten.

This is an intuitive judgment rather than a scientific process, so don't worry too much about making sure that every emotion you feel fits consistently onto the same scale. Go with your gut and understand that the first number that pops into your head will be the right number. If you prefer a different scale, such as zero to ten or one to five, feel free to use that instead.

The number you share will give whoever you're talking to valuable information about how to communicate with you. If they ask you how angry you are, and you scream "Ten!" they will know that you're triggered and might need to calm down before you can engage in a rational debate. On the other hand, if you say "two," they will know you are only mildly affected and capable of considering other points of view. This behavior should of course be calibrated to your particular temperament. The scale is relative, and some people might consider a two to be unusually angry, whereas others would experience it as completely normal.

If you and your partner regularly use this scale, you will both become more accustomed to interpreting each other's moods and learn to respond appropriately. Hopefully, this will result in fewer high-intensity experiences of anger and frustration and more of pleasure and joy.

Tool 2.19:
Empathy

Relating to how others feel.

Motivation

During arguments or heated discussions, many of us succumb to the temptation to seek out a practical solution as opposed to listening to how the other person is feeling. More often than not, this approach will fuel conflict, as people feel unseen and unheard. Recognizing their emotions is an essential part of connecting with them and perhaps moving toward a resolution.

We all respond better to others when we feel understood and feel that our emotions are valid and relevant. Empathy allows everyone to feel at ease and improves almost every conversation.

Benefits

- Connects us with others, enabling everyone to feel supported and understood.
- Can be applied even when you don't agree with the other person's point of view.
- Opens a path toward deeper conversation. Often, someone who receives empathy will be more likely to listen.

Challenges

- We may not notice others' emotionsbecause we are too wrapped up in our own.
- Deliberately acknowledging others' feelings ("I understand that you feel sad right now . . .") might feel artificial at times.

Application

One way to show empathy is through asking questions, sometimes known as empathetic guesses. These should be inquiries aimed at discovering another person's feelings. Listen carefully and try to come up with a guess or two about what your conversational partner is feeling and why. To show them that you understand what they're feeling, you may wish to describe how their emotions appear to you. Then, gently ask whether you've understood them correctly. Don't ever insist that you know what someone else is feeling—you might be wrong and end up annoying them or, worse, making them feel so misunderstood that they shut down. Instead, remain open to what they share with you.

Questions can often be more effective than direct statements because they are open-ended and don't assume that you are right—they leave more room for the other party to correct you if needed. However, try to avoid sounding like you are interrogating them. The key is to go beyond understanding purely with your brain and also to connect with your heart. Feel and express sincere curiosity—don't just pump people for information.

Questions you can ask to make an empathetic connection with someone include:

- "You seem somewhat upset. Is everything okay?"
- "Are you sad about X, or is it something else?"

If you're struggling to connect with another person, you can also share your emotional reality in a bid for their empathy:

- "I really would like to be empathetic with you right now, but it's hard because I'm frustrated myself."
- "I'd like to be fully present, but I'm currently exhausted. Can we continue this after I take a short break?"

Another essential facet of empathy is self-empathy. You are the only person in the world who can always be there for yourself, and asking for and giving self-empathy can be just as powerful as receiving it from another person. This takes practice, but it can be highly rewarding (see Tool 3.4: Talk to Your Inner Selves). Empathy is also a major component of Tool 2.1: Nonviolent Communication.

Further Reading

1. "Brené Brown on Empathy": https://youtube.com/watch?v=1Evwgu369Jw.

2. Andrea Brandt, "The Secret to a Happy Relationship Is Empathy," Psychology Today, March 3, 2020, https://psychologytoday.com/us/blog/mindful-anger/202003/the-secret-happy-relationship-is-empathy.

Tool 2.20:
The Way of the Superior Man

A spiritual guide by David Deida to help men master the challenges of women, work, and sexual desire.

Motivation

The Way of the Superior Man by David Deida is a guide for men, encouraging them to get in touch with themselves and live in alignment with their true nature.[6] The book is divided into many short chapters that cover various topics.

David Deida's approach can help men in a range of relationships, in finding their sense of purpose, and in leveling up their presence with women. Deida focuses particularly on the value of polarity, contending that the modern trend toward total equivalence between men and women is misguided and makes for stagnation in relationships. He argues that in most healthy relationships, one person will assume the masculine role while the other takes on a more feminine identity. Deida asserts that this polarity is positive and meets the needs of both parties. This principle applies even in relationships between two men or two women, and *The Way of the Superior Man* is intended for anyone who finds themselves called to the masculine role at least some of the time.

Men who are feeling stuck and having difficulty connecting with people or who are feeling drained by the expectations placed upon them may find that *The Way of the Superior Man* helps them understand themselves and show up in a stronger, more authentic way.

---

[6] David Deida, *The Way of the Superior Man: A Spiritual Guide to Mastering the Challenges of Women, Work, and Sexual Desire* (Sounds True Publishing, 2017).

Benefits

- There are many self-help books available but few stand-out texts on how to be a man in the modern world. Even if you disagree with some of Deida's perspectives, considering them will help you figure out what you *do* believe.

- Discusses deep principles such as meditation and presence (see Tool 6.1: Meditation) and provides a guide to applying them in various situations in a man's life.

- The short, stand-alone chapters make it easy to dip into the book and choose one that matches your current mood and needs.

Challenges

- Deida's worldview can be rather dogmatic and prescriptive. His opinions about the world don't leave a great deal of room for plurality.

- Some people have criticized the tone as occasionally misogynistic. With this in mind, it's worth reading the book with a critical eye.

Application

Simply read the book and find the chapters that appeal to you most. To give you examples of Deida's philosophy, many people have found the following chapters extremely insightful.

Live as If Your Father Were Dead

The idea behind this chapter is that in order to be truly free to be your own self, you must grow up and release yourself from your father's expectations, both positive and negative. You can love your father without living your life trying to live up to his standards. Ultimately, Deida says, you must make crucial life decisions based not on your father's expectations of you but on your own expectations of yourself.

Enjoy Your Friends' Criticism

According to Deida, the capacity to receive constructive criticism from friends is a measure of your masculine energy. If you can listen without becoming hurt or defensive, their feedback can help you see your true self more clearly. In this context, your friends are not there to support or constrain you but simply to help you become a better person. Your job is neither to accept nor deny their criticism but to weigh it carefully, discerning whether there is any truth in it. Then, if there's some value for you to glean, use it to improve yourself.

Own Your Darkest Desires

We all have dark thoughts and desires, which we might be tempted to deny. Deida, however, claims that this is counterproductive. When we refuse to acknowledge our darker impulses and pretend to be perfect, we deny a part of ourselves, which then plays out anyway through our subconscious. When we instead embrace these desires, we can integrate them into our psyche without allowing them to run our lives.

Turn Your Lust into Gifts

When a heterosexual man sees a beautiful woman, it is natural for him to feel sexual desire for her. In most situations, however, it's not possible to simply act on that desire. Deida recommends feeling it fully but resisting the urge to take refuge in fantasies. Instead, he suggests transmuting this energy, allowing it to circulate beyond the physical so that it finds a healthy creative outlet. This can be painting, writing, or another form of art—think of all the songs, art, and books men have created because they were inspired by beautiful women—or it can simply be a catalyst to find a higher purpose in one's work.

CHAPTER THREE

THERAPY

"Unexpressed emotions will never die. They are buried alive and will come forth later in uglier ways."

—Sigmund Freud

Just about all of us have some emotional hang-ups or mental issues that block us from being as happy as we want or from living in peace. Often, there is something we don't like about ourselves, and our inability to see and accept it only makes it worse. Perhaps we have problems maintaining friendships or close relationships, feel sad most of the time, blow up in anger without meaning to, or have issues with the shape of our body—the list of things we humans use to self-criticize is endless. Other reasons for unhappiness include habitual behaviors that don't serve us but that we're not sure how to stop such as smoking or scrolling social media. The sources of unhappiness and agitation are too numerous to list here, but one strategy for fixing them can be summed up in a single word: therapy.

Therapists work in a multitude of different ways and adhere to a broad range of philosophies, but in each case, the goal is the same: to help you figure out what you need in order to feel more satisfaction, more joy, and more peace. Based on the assumption that self-knowledge is the first step to change, therapy is not about telling you how to think or what to do. It is aimed at helping you see the hidden ways your thoughts and actions may be causing you problems.

Many of the tools in this chapter are about getting the best results from those sessions. Whether in one-on-one conversations or group settings, there are numerous ways you can optimize your results. There are also tools focused on self-improvement outside of therapeutic sessions such as Tool 3.3: Gratitude and this chapter's Pillar Tool, 3.10: Twelve Rules for Life.

It is, however, highly recommended that you explore the benefits of going to therapy, which are detailed in the first tool in this chapter.

Tool 3.1:
Go to Therapy

Try therapy to help you work through your psychological and emotional issues.

Motivation

If your relationships are difficult or you struggle to find peace in your life, you may want to consider going to a therapist. Many people find therapy to be a helpful tool for managing their stress. Additionally, people who have a mental illness such as depression, anxiety, or bipolar disorder often find that therapy is an important adjunct to their medication.

A professional therapist can help you work through your past experiences and the issues and trauma that have arisen from them. They can help you process your emotions. Many therapists also offer valuable tools and exercises that can teach you new ways to behave in situations that trouble you.

There are several different contexts in which you can see a therapist:

- **Single**: One-on-one sessions between you and your therapist.
- **Couple**: Sessions where you and your significant other attend therapy together (see Tool 3.8: Relationship Therapy).
- **Family**: When all immediate family members join in on therapy sessions (see Tool 3.8: Relationship Therapy).
- **Group**: When people affected by a common issue, such as grief or post-traumatic stress, come together and work communally with a therapist to help each other.

Starting therapy can be a difficult decision, but many people discover that, after a few sessions with the right therapist, they love it. A good therapist often becomes a trusted ally—someone who is always in your corner rooting for you. Your sessions, in turn, become safe, judgment-free zones where you can discuss whatever you need to.

Benefits

- Learning about your blind spots and growing from those insights.
- Healing emotionally and mentally from past trauma.
- Finding healthier behaviors and responses to situations.

Challenges

- It can be difficult to open up and start talking to a stranger.
- Many people are embarrassed to admit that they need help.
- It may take a long time to feel the benefits of therapy.

Application

Finding a good therapist can be challenging. You can try asking around for recommendations or browsing your local directory. Doing some research, like exploring potential therapists' websites, can give you a good feel for them and the methodologies and tools they employ. There is no substitute for an introductory meeting, where you'll get a sense of the kind of connection you might develop. You may want to ask potential therapists about their approach before meeting them. You can research it, get an idea of how it works, and evaluate whether it is suitable for you.

You will not always find your perfect therapist on the first try, so you may need to meet with a few before you find one with whom you feel safe and comfortable. Your therapy sessions may cause you to feel vulnerable, so you must feel a high level of connection with your therapist.

Sometimes, you might have doubts about whether your relationship with a therapist is working out for you. It's usually beneficial to bring these doubts up in therapy and discuss them with your therapist. Over time, if you feel your current therapist isn't the right one for you, you might want to choose a new one. There are many different schools of therapy. Some people prefer cognitive therapists, who focus on specific behavioral changes, while others prefer dynamic talk therapy, which uses the dynamics of the patient-therapist connection to investigate issues in the patient's life. Other therapies include psychoanalysis, bodywork, or breathwork. It is important not to settle when choosing a therapist. Make sure you get the right one for you.

Tool 3.2:
Lead a Purposeful Life

Knowing what you want to achieve in life gives you direction and purpose.

Motivation

When people feel adrift and don't know what to do or how to prioritize their goals, it's often because they are not tapped into a sense of purpose. It's important to know where you want to be and what you want to do. This vision of your best life and the goals you want to achieve will fuel a felt sense of purpose and generate the passion and drive you need to pursue what you want.

Benefits

- Find clarity on the life you want to live.
- Inject meaning into your day-to-day life.

Challenges

- It can be very difficult to pick up your gaze from the mundane and figure out what truly matters to you.

Application

Discovering a sense of purpose is a highly personal endeavor. People approach it in many ways, from writing exercises to vision quests to psychedelics. Providing a definitive answer to the question of how to find purpose is beyond the scope of this tool. If you're not sure what approach will work for you, don't allow the difficulty of the inquiry to lull you into inaction. Experiment. Investigate your passions. Ask yourself, "What do I want to achieve in my life?" Meditate on this question and listen to the answers that emerge. Keep in mind that you don't need to find a single, permanent answer—the inquiry itself is bound to be fruitful, and you can always repeat the process in the future to adjust or reinvent your trajectory.

The kind of answers you're seeking are concrete goals that you could feasibly attain. They are things that could be written on your tombstone. Your answers will be numerous and multifaceted because that is the nature of life. However, each part of each answer will serve as a guiding light, nudging you toward activities that match your goals and kindle your sense of purpose.

Write down the answers that come to you and keep them somewhere you can readily access them for review. Then, as you go about your day-to-day life, recall what brings you a sense of purpose and what your goals are. When you need to make decisions about your work, your personal life, and anything that has an impact on you, use these insights to provide direction.

For example, if you know you want to be physically fit as you age, you can focus on that goal to help stave off the urge to overindulge on sweets every night. If you know you want to become a medical doctor, use that point of reference to guide your schooling choices. If you know you want to retire as a very wealthy person, take the time to make financial decisions aligned with that desire.

It's helpful to review your answers at regular intervals and to check how closely your actions match your goals. You may also discover that a particular goal has lost meaning and that you want to alter your trajectory.

Further Reading

1. Jordan Peterson's Future Authoring Program: https://www.selfauthoring.com/future-authoring.
2. Nicole San Roman and Allan Stone, "The 'Why' Matters: Setting Successful Goals," University of New Mexico Health Sciences Center Newsroom, January 25, 2024, https://hsc.unm.edu/news/2024/01/setting-successful-goals.html.

Tool 3.3:
Gratitude

Cultivate an appreciation for things in your life.

Motivation

Recognizing and acknowledging people, events, and material things for which you're grateful can alleviate feelings of sadness, depression, and anxiety and bring positive feelings into your life. Intentionally practicing gratitude is a method of focusing on the good in life and can make you feel natural gratitude even when you're not practicing. Most of us have a negativity bias, and gratitude is effective in alleviating that.

Benefits

- Helps you find the positive in challenging situations.
- Creates a feedback loop of positivity.
- Enriches and bolsters your relationships.

Challenges

- Cultivating gratitude can be difficult, particularly when you need it the most (e.g., when you're depressed or anxious).
- In an attempt to exercise gratitude, you might end up faking it, which can be counterproductive.

Application

Practicing gratitude entails seeking and considering various things in your life for which you are grateful. These can be things like the people in your life and the good they bring you or your job, whether it's one that you enjoy or one that simply puts food on the table. You can be grateful for your family (however annoying they might be), for the sun's warm light, or even for the earth beneath your feet. The things you're grateful for don't need to be perfect; the key is to consider your life and find the goodness within it.

In the beginning, you'll probably practice being grateful for the good things in your life. That's often challenging enough! At more advanced levels, you can try being grateful for the difficult situations—in other words, finding the silver lining in every cloud. This skill can seem impossible, but if mastered, it can bring a surreal level of tranquility.

Practicing gratitude intentionally on a daily basis (e.g., as a nightly ritual) can profoundly improve your life. Some ways to practice gratitude include:

- **Gratitude journals:** At the end of each day or week, before you go to bed, write down three or more things for which you are thankful.

- **Gratitude meditation:** Sit in meditation and intentionally think about people, things, and events that you appreciate. Take the time to feel your gratification for them in your body. You might want to listen to one of the numerous guided gratitude meditations available online.

- **Gratitude partners:** Begin a practice where each day, you text your gratitude partner, sharing a few things that happened that you appreciate.

Further Reading

"An Antidote to Dissatisfaction": https://youtube.com/watch?v=WPPPFqsECz0.

Tool 3.4:
Talk to Your Inner Selves

A way to get in touch with the deeper parts of you.

Motivation

We all have parts of ourselves that we keep stuffed deep inside. If we don't acknowledge these different facets of ourselves, they will only become more powerful. When we are tired, scared, or otherwise low on resources, these parts can dictate how we think, speak, and act. This may mean we say things we don't intend or behave in ways that hurt ourselves or others. By getting in touch with these inner shadow selves and integrating them, we can gain better control of our lives.

This can be a process of positive dialogue and conflict resolution. By improving communication between our different parts, we can create better relationships between them, as well as between ourselves and each inner part.

Note: Some parts of ourselves are more in the light than others. This technique can be used to talk to every part of yourself, whether shadowed or otherwise.

Benefits

- The shadow parts of yourself can control your behavior. Once you access your shadow selves, you can identify them and reduce their power over you.
- As you integrate more parts of yourself, you will feel calmer and experience less internal struggle.

Challenges

- You will feel powerful resistance (for example, fear or disgust) to connecting with your shadow selves.

- Many people fear that talking to themselves is an indication of insanity or mental disturbance (although it's actually contributing to positive mental health).

- What you discover in these conversations can often be hard to digest.

Application

You can connect with your shadow selves in various ways: internal dialogue, writing, talking out loud, or even through movement.

To begin, ensure you are in a safe space where you won't be interrupted. Verbally, in writing, or in your mind, ask who wants to speak right now. Then, wait for this particular self to respond. Often it's helpful to give these characters names—you can start by asking, "Who are you?" or "What's your name?"

At first, it may not be obvious how to distinguish between yourself answering as opposed to a shadow self, but if you push through the confusion, you will feel a distinctive feeling, as if you're replying from a different "you." The inner part that replies may be a classical archetype, such as your inner child, Satan, God, or a parent, or it may be something harder to define and name. Either is okay; whatever you encounter, try to feel its unique energy and identity.

After your shadow speaks, you can respond to it and hold a conversation between the two sides. This might feel weird or awkward at first, and that's quite normal. Remember, this is a safe space, and you can fully express all parts of yourself here, just like in therapy. Some of what you discover in these sessions may scare or even disgust you, which can be hard to tolerate. Allowing yourself to feel any emotions that arise from connecting with these different parts of you can be a unique opportunity to integrate them instead of having them dictate your behavior.

Once you have a conversation going, this is your chance to ask them questions, get to know them, and express to them what's on your mind. Some questions you can try are:

- When and how were you born?
- How do you feel? What do you want or need?
- What would you like me to know about you?
- How can we reach an agreement that fulfills both of our needs?

Another way to work with your inner selves is to choose a particular topic on which you are conflicted and set a timer for thirty seconds, a minute, or more. First, talk from one point of view in a fully present, fully expressive way, uninterrupted by other parts. Warmly invite this part to share what it *does* want for you, not only what it *doesn't* want. When the timer expires, reset it and let another one of your inner selves speak its mind. This structured approach ensures all sides are heard and can facilitate better communication.

Your challenging emotions can be an excellent gateway to your shadow parts. For example, if you notice that you are judging yourself, this is a clue that, in reality, one part of yourself is judging another and that these two parts are active and accessible in that moment. Additionally, when you feel a strong emotion toward another person, such as envy or hatred, this may be an indication that a part of you is not completely realized. The envy or hatred you feel can represent an opportunity to know these parts of yourself better.

The more your different selves feel that you are considering them and the more you can reach agreements with them, the less power they will have over you. This will allow you to navigate your inner landscape with greater ease.

Your inner selves are always available to you whenever you need to communicate with them. It's important that you follow through on your agreements and adjust them as needed. Periodically, check in on your inner selves to see how they are doing and whether they need anything.

Further Reading

1. "The Jungian Shadow," The Society of Analytical Psychology, August 12, 2015, https://thesap.org.uk/articles-on-jungian-psychology-2/about-analysis-and-therapy/the-shadow/.

2. Kristeen Cherney, "Everything to Know About Your Internal Monologue," Healthline, last updated April 10, 2023, https://healthline.com/health/mental-health/internal-monologue.

3. Piotr Oles, Thomas Brinthaupt, Rachel Dier, and Dominika Polak, "Types of Inner Dialogues and Functions of Self-Talk: Comparisons and Implications," *Frontiers in Psychology* 11 (2020), https://frontiersin.org/journals/psychology/articles/10.3389/fpsyg.2020.00227/full.

4. "Voice Dialogue," GoodTherapy, last updated June 30, 2016, https://goodtherapy.org/learn-about-therapy/types/voice-dialogue#.

Tool 3.5:
Feel Your Emotions

Don't suppress emotions; allow yourself to fully experience and process them.

Motivation

Few of us are comfortable truly feeling our emotions. We find ways to ignore them, distract ourselves from them, or displace them. In many Western cultures, the idea that boys don't cry is still prevalent, which can generate the belief among men that suppressing emotions is a positive thing to do. Even those of us who aren't explicitly told to suppress our emotions grow up emulating our parents and other adults around us. If they deny their emotional reality, we internalize the idea that we need to do the same.

Unfortunately, suppressing emotions can lead to unexplained low moods and a sense of disconnection or even depression. If we lack an appreciation of our inner world, we may adopt behaviors to actively avoid our emotions. This can make us prone to negative behavior, such as outbursts of anger, social withdrawal, emotional eating, or excessive social media use. All these behaviors are rooted in an effort to numb our feelings or distract ourselves from them.

Emotions are critical to living a full life, so we need to feel them and learn to understand what they mean to us. According to the Nonviolent Communication approach, our emotions are a guide to discovering and accessing our unmet needs (see Tool 2.1: Nonviolent Communication).

Benefits

- Our emotions represent a map of our inner world. If we can't feel them, we will find it difficult to navigate our internal landscape.
- Feeling and processing suppressed emotions can have a powerful therapeutic impact.

Challenges

- Some emotions can seem too painful or scary to feel.
- Working with your emotions can take a lot of time and effort.

Application

To practice this tool, set yourself up in a situation where you won't be disturbed and have time to connect with your internal world. This could be seated meditation, a walk in nature, or somewhere else you feel comfortable. Allow yourself to feel whatever you feel, no matter how unexpected. If something upsets you, do not seek to hide it or distract yourself from it—simply feel it. Becoming aware of the sensations in your body can help here, as the wisdom of the body is a major key to accessing feelings.

Another way to connect with this tool could be with the assistance of a supportive friend. When choosing friends to explore this tool with, make sure you select those who are able to listen and offer space. Most people are in the habit of offering advice or criticism; when you're focused on feeling your emotions, you'll be in an unusually open, sensitive state and may experience this kind of feedback as hurtful. If you don't have any friends you trust to support you in this process or desire the support of someone more committed and experienced, you may want to explore it during therapy (see Tool 3.1: Go to Therapy).

Whichever methods you choose will likely require practice; you may need to try many times before you're able to actually sit with your feelings and experience them fully. If what you're feeling is particularly painful, you may be tempted to stop the process and bottle up the emotion. If you can be patient, however, and fully experience whatever arises, it will gradually dissipate, and you'll likely feel a tremendous sense of relief.

Further Reading

Guided meditation for dealing with difficult emotions: insighttimer. com/adrianaspataru/guided-meditations/dealing-with-the-difficult -the-hint-meditation.

Tool 3.6:
Talk About Therapy *in* Therapy

Openly discuss your thoughts and feelings about therapy and your therapist *with* your therapist during sessions.

Motivation

After a few therapy sessions, it's normal to discover you have developed some feelings regarding your therapist. You may feel annoyed at some behavioral quirk, a strong attraction, or even just have recurring random thoughts about them. These thoughts and feelings can be a key gateway into your therapeutic process. They often arise from transference, meaning the unconscious patterns and projections you push onto your therapist. When observed, they can be quite telling and help you make breakthroughs in your process.

Finding time and courage to raise issues that pertain directly to your therapy or therapist can be difficult, and you may be tempted to keep the conversation focused on your life outside the clinic. However, pushing through and discussing these types of issues can be very rewarding because often the same issues you experience outside (in the "there and then") will manifest directly inside the clinic (in the "here and now"). When they do, your therapist will be more than a listener or an observer; they will be a direct participant. This can allow them to see what's really going on, not just what you *think* is going on.

For the reasons above, this kind of direct interaction can be critical to the success of your therapy. A single session where you open up like this can be more beneficial than countless more traditional sessions.

Benefits

- Helps your therapist observe your relationship directly, which can give critical insight into your relationship patterns and help them adjust to your needs.
- Builds stronger bonds with your therapist, which can help you trust them more.
- Helps you develop valuable relationship and communication skills in a supportive and explorative environment.

Challenges

- This type of sharing may feel embarrassing or bring up a fear of being judged.
- Some types of information (e.g., sexual attraction, harsh criticism) can be especially difficult to share (but very therapeutically beneficial).
- Might compete with other issues you wish to discuss and seem less important, especially in short-term therapy.

Application

The first step is to identify that you have certain thoughts or feelings about your therapist. These thoughts can occur in session or in your daily life. If this happens in session, you might want to stop whatever you're talking about and share your observations. If you notice this outside of the clinic, you should either make a mental note to speak about it in your next session or even set a reminder to yourself to do so. Therapy has a way of going where *it* wants, so setting a reminder and starting the session with the topic at hand is a good way to make sure it gets discussed.

A good way to start is to let your therapist know that you have something uncomfortable to share. Before you do this, you might be worried that your therapist will become hurt, alarmed, or judgmental.

You can share this concern with them to see if they can reassure you that they're going to both handle it and be gentle with you. Experienced therapists have a variety of tools to professionally handle even the harshest feedback with dignity and responsibility.

Next, it's best to just do it: Simply say what's on your mind, without filters. After you expose your heart, a good therapist will know how to treat what you've shared with respect, discuss it with you in a way that honors your vulnerability, and use it to pave a therapeutic path forward.

If your therapist responds in a way that's uncomfortable for you, that might mean one of two things. Either this is a normal part of the therapeutic process, which doesn't always feel comfortable, or your therapist might be reacting to their own unconscious issues and projections. This countertransference can manifest in behaviors such as excessive criticism and unsolicited advice giving. While it's not always easy to distinguish between the two, trusting yourself is an important guide in this process. Even though your therapist is responsible for directing this process, it is your responsibility to set boundaries with them and ultimately to decide which therapist is right for you.

Further Reading

1. "Transference," Wikipedia, https://en.wikipedia.org/wiki/Transference.

2. "Countertransference," Wikipedia, https://en.wikipedia.org/wiki/Countertransference.

3. D. W. Winnicott, "The Use of an Object and Relating Through Identifications," Scribd, https://www.scribd.com/document/521663424/Winnicott-the-Use-of-an-Object.

Tool 3.7:
Make the Most of Therapy

Therapy is precious, so do everything you can to protect that time.

Motivation

You're in therapy for a reason. Time spent in sessions is special and important for your process. You're investing a lot of money, time, and emotional energy in therapy, so why not make the most of it?

Benefits

- Starting your session on time, without interruptions from calls and messages, can help you stay focused and present.
- Taking a few moments with yourself after you leave therapy can help you absorb and integrate everything that happened during the session.

Challenges

- This habit requires a level of discipline that can be hard to achieve, especially the first few times you apply it.
- Commitments to yourself are notoriously hard to keep. As much as you want to arrive early for sessions, the mind will play tricks and distract you.

Application

Here are a few practical tips to help you enhance your session:

- Arrive ahead of time and use that time to prepare for therapy. Think about your week, your highs and lows, the previous session, and what you want to discuss. If any troublesome topics come to mind, now might be a good time to look at them again.

- On or before your arrival, disconnect. Don't get distracted by your phone and the outside world (see Tool 1.3: Disconnect).
- During your session, dedicate your full attention to the process (e.g., don't look at your phone).
- After your session is over, take a few moments to let what happened sink in before jumping back into your day.

Tool 3.8:
Relationship Therapy

Explore interpersonal dynamics in therapy.

Motivation

There are several contexts in which therapy involving more than one person can be beneficial. The most common is couples therapy, which focuses on the dynamics between a couple and requires the participation of both partners. We depend on our attachments to others for our emotional and other needs, and when they malfunction, it can cause us great pain. Couples therapy can be an opportunity to heal wounds sustained in current or previous relationships.

In family therapy, all or most family members attend therapy together. This form of therapy is relatively rare since it requires significant investments of time and energy. However, it can be quite fruitful. As children, our psyche is forged in our families of origin, and confronting that dynamic in a safe space can unravel traumatic responses and bring profound healing.

Benefits

- Acting out relationship dynamics in a clinical setting can reveal truths that are easy to hide in solo therapy and offer opportunities to work on them directly.
- Provides a rare chance to improve your significant relationships.
- Benefits extend beyond the couple—e.g., children do better in school when Mom and Dad aren't fighting.

Challenges

- Other participants must agree to attend therapy without coercion.

- Many people resist examining the dynamics of their relationships closely for fear of what they might discover.

Application

Similar to Tool 3.1: Go to Therapy, it's important to do your research so you can find a therapist with whom both you and your spouse or family resonate. As in one-to-one therapy, there are many different styles of couples and family therapy. You may need to experiment with more than one therapist and explore different disciplines until you find one with whom you're aligned.

In most cases, family or spousal therapy is initiated by a specific event. It could be a significant conflict—such as one partner having an affair—or a close family member passing away. Whatever the reason, everyone involved must be willing to recognize the need to explore relationship dynamics that have previously remained unspoken. This can be tricky, as many people resist looking closely at themselves.

Be advised that starting relationship therapy may initially feel more painful than continuing with things as they are as hidden layers of emotion rise to the surface and repressed conflicts are expressed. This is part of the process, and a skilled therapist will know how to navigate these turbulent waters and guide the participants toward safety.

The goal of the therapist in these settings is not to solidify relationships, save marriages, or create a loving family. Instead, their objective is to enable people to fully express themselves and understand each other so they can work together more harmoniously—or, if need be, break apart and walk separate paths. To do this, many will split people into subgroups, such as parents and children. To create a safe space in these situations, they will maintain separate confidentiality agreements for each subgroup.

The duration of the work depends on the complexity of the challenges you want to work through. It usually takes more than one session, but it doesn't always continue indefinitely as personal therapy may. As a guide, you should continue the therapy sessions as long as you feel that the energy in the room is strong and that you're doing important work. When that sensation is no longer present, it's possible you may have reached the end of the usefulness of the therapy, at least for now. Or you may have simply gone as far as you can with a particular therapist and need to engage a new one.

Tool 3.9:
Coaching

Engage a coach to support you in reaching important goals.

Motivation

Coaching differs from therapy. Whereas the role of a therapist is to help you untangle your emotional challenges, find peace, and become happier, a coach has a more focused role—to guide and support you in a specific area of life. A business coach will guide you in the creation and growth of a successful career, for example, while a personal trainer (a type of coach) will push you toward your physical goals.

You can find coaches who specialize in almost anything. When you want to improve an aspect of your life, a coach may be a more appropriate choice than a therapist. Rather than exploring your emotional responses, a coach will concentrate on improving your skills and mindset and supporting you to become the person you want to be.

Benefits

- Engaging a coach can help you make progress with specific projects or goals.
- Knowing someone has your back boosts your motivation and speeds up your development.

Challenges

- Coaching is much more loosely regulated than therapy. Although there are some certifications, anyone can call themselves a coach, which can make it hard to know who offers a high-quality service.
- If it's hard to pinpoint your exact goals, coaching may not be effective.

Application

First, determine what you're seeking help with. A good therapist will help you unravel the most complex emotional blocks, even if you don't understand them yourself, but that's not really the job of a coach. While your coach should address issues that are holding you back, they are there to help you set and reach goals of your choosing. So, you'll need to identify those goals before you hire them or home in on them in the first few sessions.

Do you need a career coach to win a promotion or find a new position? A financial coach who will assist you in managing your finances more effectively? Maybe you want to learn a musical instrument, improve your acting skills, or become a better singer. There are coaches who can support you in all of these areas.

Just like finding the right therapist, choosing a coach is a matter of research and resonance. Do they have the skills you need, and do you feel comfortable putting yourself in their hands? The field is even broader than the therapeutic field, and not every coach is qualified. There are no mandatory certifications for calling oneself a coach. To determine whether a coach is reputable, you may want to perform your due diligence by researching their reputation online and perhaps asking to speak to current or previous clients for references.

Once you get into a coaching relationship, commit to getting as much as possible out of it—after all, you're paying for your coach's time and expertise. If they give you homework, try and complete it to the best of your ability. If you're struggling or if you don't understand the relevance of something your coach asks you to do, be open with them. This will help them help you. To assess your progress and ensure you're on track, it's a good idea to track and review your goals on a regular basis and possibly adapt them as needed.

Tool 3.10:
ⅈ Twelve Rules for Life

A selection of principles for navigating chaos from Jordan Peterson.

Motivation

Over the past few decades, the human race has experienced a general movement toward greater freedom, including freedom from restrictive monarchies, from the autocratic rule of tyrants, and from the dictates of religion. According to Jordan Peterson, author of *12 Rules for Life*, this overall trend is positive, but in the process, we have lost some of the grounding that previously stabilized our lives.[7]

In a postmodern world, we may find it difficult to identify and hold on to strong moral values. This can be especially true for atheists, who often struggle to find meaning and grapple with nihilism. Without values and principles to anchor us, the world can look excessively chaotic. Adopting some rules can help tip the scales in the other direction, fashioning order from the chaos.

Benefits

- These rules can be a shining beacon to those who have lost their way in the world or provide a burst of clarity to anyone.

- Peterson encourages us to confront the truth about our lives, taming the metaphorical dragons that might otherwise grow, fester, and devour us.

- The writing is rich and worthy of reflection. Diving into the content drives the point home and allows the lessons to penetrate deeper layers of the psyche in unexpected ways.

---

[7] Jordan Peterson, *12 Rules for Life: An Antidote for Chaos* (Random House, Canada, 2018).

Challenges

- The rules are simple, but implementing them is not easy. They require us to step off the path of least resistance and make painful changes to our lives.
- Many of us place a high value on freedom and may resist the very concept of following rules advocated by someone else.
- At times, Peterson's writing style may appear impenetrable. Sticking with it and experiencing the full value requires a lot of patience.

Application

In *12 Rules for Life,* rules that initially appear straightforward and even obvious in their short form reveal surprising depths of meaning when explored in their entirety. The book can be a tough read, but it's worth persevering. Peterson's writing style sometimes appears to meander, taking the reader in unexpected directions as he shares stories, parables, and proverbs that initially seem irrelevant. Stick with him, however, and the payoff is worth the effort.

Fundamentally, Peterson's message is that in order to build a rich and meaningful life, we have an obligation to do good, improving ourselves and the world around us. This is never easy, so we should be prepared to embrace struggle as a core component of human existence. In other words, overcoming challenges is part of what makes living worthwhile and is the only path to a true sense of accomplishment.

There is considerable value in reading the entire book. For the purposes of this tool, however, we will summarize all twelve of the tools and dive into three of the most important in greater detail.

1. Stand up straight with your shoulders back.

This rule is arguably the basis for all the others. By standing up straight with our shoulders back, we indicate to ourselves and others that we are ready to take on the world and show ourselves in the best possible light.

2. Treat yourself like someone you are responsible for helping.

This tool is about giving yourself the same care, kindness, and attention that you would show to a loved one in need of your support. This means prioritizing self-care and self-respect, acknowledging your needs, and doing your best to support yourself.

3. Make friends with people who want the best for you.

Surrounding ourselves with those who inspire growth and bring positivity into our lives is essential to better relationships, greater happiness, and more well-being. By the same token, it's important not to weave negative people into our lives.

4. Compare yourself to who you were yesterday, not to who someone else is today.

It's easy to compare ourselves with others. It's far healthier and more productive, however, to concentrate on where we have come from and how much progress we've made.

5. Do not let your children do anything that makes you dislike them.

Peterson contends that children who don't receive corrective feedback early in life have a much greater chance of developing into poorly socialized adults with issues respecting their own boundaries and those of others. Therefore, teaching your children how to behave is a kindness to them and to everyone they interact with.

6. Set your house in perfect order before you criticize the world.

In Peterson's view, while we can rail against society, the government, or God, there is more agency and autonomy in focusing on our sphere of influence and changing the things that are within our power.

7. **Pursue what is meaningful (not what is expedient).**

   Meaning is usually not found in fleeting pleasure but rather in doing things that match our deeper values. Expediency consists of doing the obvious, easy thing, even when that results in storing up problems for later. Life satisfaction stems from considering the broader impact of our actions on our future selves, our families, and society at large.

8. **Tell the truth—or at least don't lie.**

   In the short term, it may seem as though lies keep us safe from pain, but in the long term, we pay the price by losing our authenticity and inviting chaos into our lives. Peterson says we should strive to resist this self-deception and find the courage to be who we truly are (see Tool 2.7: Radical Honesty).

9. **Assume the person you are listening to might know something you don't.**

   It helps to remember that, however much we think we know, our conversational partners usually know at least a few things we don't. Therefore, we can certainly learn from them if we have the curiosity and patience to keep our ears open.

10. **Be precise in your speech.**

    Many of us live with undefined problems and use vague language as a way to avoid confronting them directly. When we articulate the precise issues—what Peterson calls "naming the dragon"—we are in a better position to overcome them.

11. **Do not bother children while they are skateboarding.**

    Peterson believes that children learn crucial life lessons when they experiment with chaos and danger in unsupervised environments. Skateboarding is an example of this type of environment—an activity where they can take risks, succeed and fail, and improve their capabilities.

12. Pet a cat when you encounter one in the street.

Life can be extremely hard, even for those of us in prosperous nations. Therefore, we shouldn't pass up the opportunity to appreciate small moments of happiness and levity, such as befriending an animal.

*   *   *

There's a great deal more to say about all these rules, but hopefully, these brief summaries provide you with food for thought and inspire you to explore the rules that you find most interesting. Now, to give a deeper perspective, let's dive a little more into three of them.

1. Stand up straight with your shoulders back.

In this tool, Peterson discusses the urge to move up social hierarchies. He argues that this drive is fundamental and has existed for hundreds of millions of years, embedded in most animal species, including humans.

Like it or not, we should recognize this core motivation in ourselves. As a species, we naturally create hierarchies and consistently strive to climb the ladder (usually multiple ladders). We do this not necessarily by confronting one another directly but by increasing our fitness, wealth, social status, and even personal awareness, boosting characteristics that denote dominance and attractiveness.

In Peterson's view, while there can be negatives to hierarchical thinking, it's impossible to eliminate it. The drive for self-improvement and advancement can be a powerful motivator, so we should adopt it rather than fight against it.

2. Pursue what is meaningful (not what is expedient).

When we reflect on the vastness of time, it's easy to feel that our lives are insignificant, made up of just fleeting moments in a timeline that stretches beyond comprehension. This can tempt us to focus on short-term pleasures and avoid life's struggles, believing our choices have little lasting impact. Yet, deep down, we know that not all actions are equal. Helping others, contributing to something greater than ourselves, or even simply growing as individuals resonates more deeply than momentary distractions.

Peterson argues that while expediency—doing what feels good now—offers temporary relief, it doesn't fulfill us in the long run. What truly sustains us is the pursuit of meaning. This might look like sacrificing leisure to invest in your future, standing up for what you believe is right, or offering support to someone in need. Though meaning can be difficult to define, we all feel its presence when our actions align with something larger than ourselves. It's this alignment that brings genuine, lasting satisfaction, making the hard path worthwhile.

3. **Assume the person you are listening to might know something you don't.**

Conversation is how we organize our minds. It's extremely difficult to both talk and listen to ourselves, so we benefit greatly from sharing our thoughts with people we trust and receiving their honest feedback.

This type of conversation sometimes invites others to listen to us and sometimes requires us to play the role of listener, paying attention to what someone else is sharing with us and, when they're ready, giving them our feedback. Listening well involves developing the capacity to understand what others are saying without leaping to conclusions, judging them, or forcing our point of view upon them.

Another element of becoming a good listener is accepting that others, with their unique perspectives, know things that we don't. Even if they don't have unique subject knowledge, they know what *they* are thinking and feeling about the conversation, which may hold valuable insights. It's a good practice to approach every conversation with this awareness in mind.

Summary

Whatever your current circumstances, at least a few of these twelve rules probably contain some wisdom you can apply. While the summaries here are no substitute for reading the full book, they may provide a spark of inspiration. If the rules resonate with you, review them occasionally and see whether they can lighten your life a little.

Tool 3.11:
Explore Your Different Identities

Delve inside to discover and reframe
your sense of self.

Motivation

We all identify with particular aspects of our personalities or roles we play in life. For example, you may see yourself as smart, funny, or shy. You may define yourself as a husband, a wife, a father, or a mother, or you may define yourself by your wealth or achievements.

These identities act as shorthand descriptions of who you are, enabling you to communicate effectively with others and function in the world. On the other hand, sometimes you may hold on to identities that once represented your true self but that no longer feel authentic to you. You can outgrow identities in the same way that children outgrow clothing, but you won't always realize it's happening. You may even make a split-second decision that reshapes your self-definition.

Another possibility is that you confuse transient traits with core identities, building them into your personality and experiencing them as parts of yourself. If you say, "I am depressed," for example, it becomes strongly associated with who you believe yourself to be. However, if you say, "I have depression," it occurs as a diagnosis of a condition, one that is temporary and can be fixed.

By examining the characteristics and descriptors you habitually apply to yourself, you can discover which ones are still relevant and which ones require updating. You may even wish to drop some completely. By the same token, it's possible to use this tool to discover new roles or personality traits you'd like to embody more frequently or fully.

Benefits

- Develop a more thorough idea of who you are, who you want to be, and who you don't want to be.

- This exercise can bring a feeling of clarity and lightness and serve as an anchor.

Challenges

- Examining your sense of identity can feel vulnerable, even threatening, if you find yourself questioning cherished identities.

- Your critical mind may revolt and tell you this is useless or nonsensical.

Application

Begin by preparing a pen and paper, setting aside some time, and finding a quiet place where you won't be disturbed. It's possible to use a computer or a phone for this exercise, but cutting yourself off from electronic stimuli and writing your responses is likely to yield deeper self-reflection and more profound insights. Ask yourself, "Who am I?" and wait for answers to form in your mind. What words, titles, or descriptions appear in your consciousness?

As possible answers make themselves known to you, write them down, even—perhaps especially—if they seem weird or surprising. As you write each one, take a moment and allow yourself to feel the emotional content of the words. What feelings do you associate with each one?

When you feel that you've emptied yourself of all the descriptors, review the list and select a few that stand out as most fundamental to your core sense of identity. Take a good look at each one and examine your relationship with them. For example, if you consider yourself smart, how do you relate to your intelligence? Do you have a need to prove your cleverness or see yourself as superior to others because of it?

And if so, can you loosen your grip on this characteristic? What emotions does the thought *I am smart* arouse in you? Who would you be without this title? What if you were stupid? What would that mean about you? Give yourself time to explore these questions.

Next, you can select a few that you'd like to experience more deeply. For these traits, ask yourself how you can best do this. Look for concrete actions you can take. If you'd like to deepen your relationship with fatherhood, for example, how can you spend more meaningful time with your children? Should you take a parenting course? Discuss options with your spouse? Or simply take your children to the park this afternoon?

This process can give you a different perspective on the core components of your identity. You may discover that your identity is not just a bunch of self-prescribed titles but that you can embody a range of roles and characteristics without any of them ultimately defining who you are. This can be deeply freeing and a stepping stone on the road to generating change.

Further Reading

1. Charles Freligh, "Therapy Toolkit: Move From Fear To Fearless, Lesson 9," InsightTimer, https://insighttimer.com/meditation-courses/course_charles-frelighs-course-form.

2. BetterHelp Editorial Team, "Exploring Some of the Most Common Personality Traits," BetterHelp, last updated October 21, 2024, https://www.betterhelp.com/advice/personality/what-are-the-most-common-personality-traits/.

3. Take personality quizzes, like the Myers-Briggs Type Indicator, to help you explore some of your characteristics.

CHAPTER FOUR

BODY

"Take care of your body. It's the only place you have to live."

—Jim Rohn

This chapter is concerned with your physical body, in particular with your diet and activity. We all want a healthy and attractive physique, and the desire to attain this often serves as a motivating factor behind changes in the way we eat or exercise. But the value of taking care of the body is far more than just cosmetic; appropriate movement and nutrition will improve all the other facets of life, supporting all the other tools in this book.

You will find tools here to help you find the motivation to work out or assist you in choosing more interesting ways of getting the exercise you need, along with quick activities you can engage in when you don't have a lot of time to spare. There are also tools that support you in sticking with a diet or nutrition plan and ideas about finding the right plan for you.

We all know we need to eat healthily and lose some pounds if we're overweight, but there are endless ideas about what good nutrition looks like. Equally, we all understand that in an era when most of us sit at a desk for several hours a day, regular exercise is important. This intellectual knowledge, however, may not be enough to actually get us moving. It can be very difficult to make ourselves do the things we feel we should do, even when the reward is improved health. We may blame our busy schedules for feeling like we don't have time for the extra shopping and cooking required to eat healthy meals or for working out at the gym. If this describes your situation, take heart; many of the tools in these pages are aimed at helping you fit exercise and good nutrition into the most packed schedule. They open with HIIT—a brief, high-intensity workout routine and the first tool in the Body chapter.

Tool 4.1:
High-Intensity Interval Training (HIIT)

Exercise in short, highly intensive bursts.

Motivation

For many people, time is one of the biggest impediments to working out. They feel that they cannot find thirty to sixty minutes (plus travel time) to exercise. Others struggle to find the energy and motivation to be physically active.

An easier alternative to long training sessions comes in the form of high-intensity interval training (HIIT)—highly intense workout sessions lasting just a few minutes that can fit into almost any schedule. HIIT sessions are generally no more than ten minutes long; if you're terribly short on time, even regular one- to two-minute sessions can be beneficial.

HIIT as a general exercise methodology, as well as several of its variants, have been studied extensively and found to provide significant health benefits, including improvements in cardiovascular health, insulin sensitivity, body composition, and aerobic and anaerobic fitness.

Benefits

- A great way to create a new workout habit—it's easier to commit to seven minutes than to thirty.
- HIIT is designed to be accessible in your home or office and doesn't require a visit to the gym.
- Provides all the regular benefits of exercise: increases muscle strength, burns fat, improves cardiovascular health, and boosts mood.

Challenges

- Like any new habit, it takes effort to start and maintain.
- While the exercises may be done in short bursts, they are still tough, especially if you're not used to exercising.
- May not be suitable for some people. You should discuss with your physician whether you are a good candidate for this style of exercise.

Application

Probably the best way to explore HIIT is to browse YouTube and find a workout video to try out. There are many options of varying lengths aimed at everyone from beginners to more advanced athletes. HIIT comes in many guises and subcategories, such as Tabata, EMOM (every minute on the minute), AMRAP (as many reps as possible), and more. You might want to experiment with a few different styles until you find one that matches your goals, stamina, and allotted time, and either pick one type to focus on or mix them up. You can even pick a single video you like and exercise with it every time. Don't spend too much time debating this; just try out a few and see what works.

Fundamentally, all these forms of HIIT follow a similar pattern: a set time performing reps of a particular exercise followed by a brief rest period, then by another exercise, and so on. Tabata, for example, comprises twenty seconds of work, then ten seconds of rest. The exercises vary from strength training techniques like squats and crunches to aerobic techniques like jumping jacks and jogging in place. Regardless of the specific style, the goal of this type of training is to work your body as hard as you can during the exercise intervals and then rest in between, squeezing a lot of intensity into a brief time period.

Further Reading

1. Muhammed Mustafa Atakan, Yanchun Li, Sükran Nazan Kosar, Hüseyin Hüsrev Turnagöl, and Xu Yan, "Evidence-Based Effects of High-Intensity Interval Training on Exercise Capacity and Health: A Review with Historical Perspective," *International Journal of Environmental Research and Public lic* 18, no. 13 (July 5, 2021): 7201, https://www.mdpi.com/1660-4601/18/13/7201.

2. The Nutrition Source, "HIIT (High-Intensity Interval Training)," Harvard T.H. Chan School of Public Health, last reviewed November 2021, https://nutritionsource.hsph.harvard.edu/high-intensity-interval-training/.

3. Stephanie Watson, "7-Minute Workout," *Web*MD, September 13, 2023, https://webmd.com/fitness-exercise/a-z/seven-minute-workout.

4. "7 Minute Workout Song": https://youtube.com/watch?v=mmq5zZfmIws.

Tool 4.2:
Find Physical Activities You Enjoy

Break through the boredom of exercising by picking styles you find intrinsically satisfying.

Motivation

Some people find that going to a gym or working with a trainer is boring, and they suffer through it for the sake of their health goals. For those people, finding an alternative physical activity that they enjoy can transform their exercise experience and significantly boost their motivation to work out.

Benefits

- Obviously, enjoying exercise beats suffering through it.
- You're more likely to sustain a habit that you like.

Challenges

- For some people, the thought of finding exercise pleasurable seems impossible.
- You may have to experiment a bit until you find a style that works for you.

Application

Exercise is supposed to be challenging. However, doing challenging things can be fun, or it can feel like a drag. If, over time, you notice that you're not enjoying your workouts and counting the minutes and seconds until the sessions end, you might want to try switching it up a bit.

First, consider modifying your current workout. You could try changing the duration and intensity (see Tool 4.1: High-Intensity

Interval Training (HIIT)), working out with a friend or a trainer, listening to podcasts or music, or even calling a friend for companionship during the session. If none of these options help, you can try changing to another form of exercise entirely.

Some alternative exercises you can try:

- Martial arts
- Climbing
- Mountain biking or hiking
- Playing in a sports league
- Virtual reality games (boxing or music games are popular)

Each possibility offers unique benefits. With martial arts, for example, the excitement and challenge of facing off against a rival can be quite stimulating, whereas mountain biking can offer fresh air and beautiful scenery. There are hundreds of options to explore, depending on your preferences, abilities, and location.

The key is to find something you truly enjoy that requires some kind of physical stamina and do it every week. In between, you can supplement your workout with running, weight training, or training that will support the sport you enjoy. Regardless of the activity you choose, try to show up with a positive disposition. Remember, you've chosen to exercise and work toward your health goals—that attitude alone can bring a sense of intrinsic satisfaction to any workout.

Tool 4.3:
Hack Your Workout Routine

Plan your day-to-day life to squeeze in extra exercise.

Motivation

It's easy to get stuck in a workout rut. You do the same exercises every day or run the same distance, and before long, your performance starts to plateau. You could train longer or harder, but it may not be easy for you to find extra time in your schedule or the energy you need to push beyond your existing limits.

Even within tight time or energy constraints, however, there are various ways you can add physical movements to your day, thus improving your strength and stamina, clearing your mind, and boosting your vitality. You might not have time to go to the gym, but you can focus instead on moving your body within the constraints of your daily routine and finding little moments to exercise even on a busy day.

Benefits

- Packs more workout time into your schedule.
- Spreads the benefits of exercise throughout your day.
- Keeps exercise feeling fun and novel.

Challenges

- Like all exercise, starting and persisting with a new routine requires willpower.
- Filling spare moments with activity can become exhausting.

Application

Even if your days are quite busy, there's a good chance you can find ways to build more exercise into your schedule. Sometimes, this may be a case of substituting one activity for another—for example, replacing your normal desk with a standing desk or a treadmill desk. Another option that falls into this category is walking or cycling to work instead of driving. At other times, it may involve using a few minutes of idle time to do something physical. You could install a pull-up bar in your doorframe, for example, and do a set of pull-ups when you break after a twenty-five-minute Pomodoro session (see Tool 1.4: The Pomodoro Technique).

There are countless ways to slip more activity into your day. When you go to the store, park at the opposite end of the street or the farthest corner of the parking lot and walk the difference. Pace while you're on the phone or during meetings. Take the stairs instead of the elevator. If you work on a high floor of an office building, you can turn this into a game, getting off the elevator one floor early, then two, then three, steadily increasing the distance you walk as your fitness improves. You can clear some room in your workspace and do a set of push-ups at regular intervals during the day—or play your favorite tune and dance.

Individually, these small shifts may seem insignificant, but their impact builds incrementally. If you make a habit of always choosing the more active option and make small additions to your exercise routine where possible, you will soon see the benefits begin to rack up.

Tool 4.4:
Breathe Before Eating

Become present prior to meals to increase your agency around food.

Motivation

This tool, along with the following five (Tools 4.5: If You Diet, Do It Sustainably to 4.9: Agree to Be Hungry), all focus on your relationship with food and nutrition. Each one takes a different angle, from choosing sustainable dieting practices to thinking carefully about what foods you keep in the house to allowing yourself to be hungry at times without immediately succumbing to the desire to eat. The third angle is the most fundamental.

At times, we all eat without thinking. You may be at a large event with an overabundance of food, so you eat without stopping to check whether you're actually hungry and whether you want to put the particular foods on offer inside your body. At other times, you may eat when you're bored, sad, or stressed in an unconscious effort to distract yourself from those difficult emotions. These knee-jerk reactions can undermine your relationship with food. If you're dieting, they may prevent you from making progress. Even if they're not, they may spoil your enjoyment and your health.

Finding ways to limit this type of mindless eating can be very beneficial, and taking a few deep breaths before making the decision to put something in your mouth is a valuable first step.

Benefits

- Gain greater awareness and decision-making skills about your eating habits.
- Helps you remain on course with your diet or weight goals.

Challenges

- The conditioned urge to eat whatever is available can be strong and hard to overcome.
- In social situations, taking the time to breathe for a few seconds can feel awkward.

Application

Wherever you are, whenever you are about to eat something, take a moment to stop and become present. Whether you're out at a party, about to tuck into a favorite meal at home, or standing in front of a vending machine on your work break, the principle is the same. Stop, breathe, and check in with your mental and physical state.

Take a few deep breaths and investigate the sensations in your mind and body. Are you really hungry? Or are you about to eat due to habit, boredom, or social pressure? Will the food you're about to eat satisfy your hunger, or will it just distract you from your immediate circumstances?

Take enough time to allow a truthful answer to emerge. Then, if you determine that the food will meet your needs, allow yourself to eat. Otherwise, if you're not hungry, and you realize the food you're contemplating will not fulfill any need, you can choose to support your higher goals and restrain yourself.

To make it easier to resist temptation, it can be useful to prime yourself with a few other options. Carry healthy snacks with you so you feel less pressure to eat whatever is available. Get into the habit of drinking plenty of water, which can quench both your thirst and feelings of hunger. Distract yourself from the desire to eat by doing something else, such as going for a walk. You can also practice mindfulness, mentally acknowledging your hunger whenever you feel it. These steps can help you feel more in control of your choices.

Tool 4.5:
If You Diet, Do It Sustainably

Choose a style of eating that you can continue indefinitely.

Motivation

Diet culture is everywhere, but many diets are aimed at short-term results rather than long-term health. Many people lose a little weight, then find that they can't sustain their dieting habits due to insatiable hunger or emotional factors. If you do decide to choose a diet, picking a way of eating that you're able to continue for years rather than weeks or months gives you a much better chance of losing weight at a healthy pace—and keeping it off.

Generally, we all know the best foods for us to eat, but our choices don't always reflect that knowledge. It may be that we get in the habit of eating convenient fast food, or we try a fad diet and—after the initial weight loss—find it difficult to maintain. At this point, many people regain whatever weight they lost—and even more. Instead, it's better to think strategically and pick long-term, realistic goals.

Benefits

- By concentrating on sustainability, you set yourself up to stick with a diet and attain key long-term health goals.
- Building habits that support overall well-being develops a sense of ownership and accountability around food.

Challenges

- Quick-fix diets are tempting for a reason—they promise rapid change. Dieting sustainably requires the discipline to reject the promise of miraculous results in favor of slow and steady progress.

- Maintaining motivation over the long term can be tough, especially when weight loss is slow or plateaus.

Application

When evaluating a new eating plan, approach it systematically by first assessing its compatibility with your existing lifestyle rather than trying to entirely reshape your life around the diet. To do this, consider the following steps:

1. **Identify your personal dietary preferences and needs:** Make a list of foods you enjoy—and want to keep eating—and those you dislike, along with any dietary restrictions you have due to health conditions or personal beliefs.

2. **Assess the diet's restrictions and allowances:** Does it ban foods you love? Does it allow foods you dislike? Is it flexible enough to accommodate your lifestyle?

3. **Establish a plan for setbacks:** Despite your best efforts, there may be days when you deviate from your chosen diet. Rather than viewing this as a failure, have a plan in place to handle such instances. This could include healthier substitutes for your cravings or a strategy to get back on track after a slipup.

4. **Secure a support system:** Connect with someone you can reach out to when following your chosen plan is tough. This could be a friend, spouse, therapist, or even a support group. This kind of support system can provide motivation, accountability, and advice when things get challenging.

For instance, if you have a sweet tooth, a low-carbohydrate diet might not be sustainable for you. Instead, consider a plan that allows for a moderate intake of sugar. Similarly, if you enjoy fried foods but have high cholesterol, find a diet that incorporates healthy oils and cholesterol-lowering foods. Remember, the goal is to find a balance that ensures you get both nutritional value and satisfaction from your meals.

Tool 4.6:
Remove Temptations

Set up an environment that supports your diet.

Motivation

If you love sweets and you open your refrigerator only to be faced with a piece of cake, at some point, you're going to eat it, especially if you're on a diet that restricts carbs. Similarly, if you go out to eat and a dessert arrives at the table, along with several spoons and plates so everyone can share, you will most likely indulge.

The human brain responds to immediate stimuli—what you see, you will want. To increase your sense of agency around food rather than succumb to instinctively eating whatever you crave, remove temptations from your environment.

Benefits

- Creating barriers against tempting foods fosters a greater sense of control and agency over your eating habits.
- Increases your chances of sticking to your diet and achieving your health goals.

Challenges

- This tactic isn't foolproof. You can always get around it by simply picking up the phone and ordering pizza.
- In some circumstances, you will need the cooperation of others.

Application

A good way to reduce access to tempting foods is to stock your kitchen mindfully—for example, by choosing not to buy certain foods and bring them into your home. This can keep foods you don't wish to eat out of your reach. If you live with other people, however, this may not always be easy or feasible. In this case, you may ask them to keep their sweets and snacks in the laundry room or in a secret drawer, off-limits to you, to keep them out of your sight and mind. Alternatively, ask whether they can keep them at the back of the refrigerator, behind the freshly washed, ready-to-eat fruits.

When you eat out and find that your appetite doesn't match what you've ordered, you may keep eating anyway. To combat this tendency, push your plate a little farther away from you to give yourself a signal that you're done, or simply ask the waiter to box up what's left and take it to go.

If you're in a group of people who are sharing dessert, let the waiter know you don't want to participate and that they should not bring an extra plate and utensils for you to use. (Be prepared to fight off persistent waiters!) Another option is excusing yourself to go for a quick walk while others are eating dessert.

Further Reading

1. "Creating a Healthy Eating Environment," Digestive Care Center, March 24, 2016, https://dccevv.com/2016/03/creating-healthy-eating-environment/.

2. "How to Build an Environment That Supports Your Goals + Helps You Get 'In Control' of Your Cravings," Vitality Nutrition (blog), June 7, 2022, https://vitalitynutrition.ca/blog/how-to-build-an-environment-that-supports-your-goals-get-in-control-of-your-cravings.

Tool 4.7:
Nutritional Supplements

Consume extra nutrients in pill or capsule form.

Motivation

Even if you make a considerable effort to eat healthily, studies show that the food we eat today is less nutrient-dense than the food eaten by our ancestors. When you're working to improve your health and want a little boost to your existing efforts, supplements can fill that gap. They're extra weapons in the arsenal of tools you can call on to achieve your health goals.

Supplements can be helpful to fill in gaps in your diet or lifestyle. Many of us don't eat enough vegetables, ingest the right amount of iron, or consume enough essential vitamins like B12 or D. When you know you're not eating as many vegetables or fresh fruits as you should, for whatever reason, you can take them in pill form.

This is especially true when you don't have the time or energy to locate healthy food. You may be traveling or in an especially busy period of your life, with little time to cook meals with fresh ingredients. While not a perfect solution, supplementation can compensate, at least to some degree, for nutrients you're not getting through your diet.

Benefits

- Increased vitality, greater energy, and improved overall health.
- A convenient way to ingest a lot of nutrients.

Challenges

- Many people are hesitant to trust the efficacy of supplements.
- Determining the most appropriate options can be confusing.

Application

There is no one-size-fits-all rule to selecting and taking supplements. It's important to take advice from the most reliable sources you can find because there's a lot of conflicting information on what works, what doesn't, and what's safe. For the best results, consider consulting a physician or nutritional specialist who can run tests revealing where you may be deficient and what supplements are likely to be most beneficial for you.

There's a huge range of supplements available, and it's up to you to determine which ones are most suited to your needs and lifestyle. A pregnant woman, for example, will benefit from different supplements than a teenager who refuses to eat their greens.

As a general guideline, however, you may wish to start with a good-quality multivitamin and a source of omega-3 fatty acids, which are essential for brain health and are frequently deficient in modern diets. Vitamin C may help if you have a cold, whereas vitamin D can be invaluable in cold climates, where you may not get enough exposure to the rays of the sun. If you're lifting weights and trying to build muscle, you'll probably wish to take some form of protein supplementation. This is not an exhaustive list—you should consult someone regarding your particular situation.

Further Reading

1. Rachel Lovell, "How Modern Food Can Regain Its Nutrients," BBC, https://bbc.com/future/bespoke/follow-the-food/why-modern-food-lost-its-nutrients/.

2. Bárbara Pinho, "Is Modern Food Lower In Nutrients?" Chemistry World, December 5, 2023, https://chemistryworld.com/features/is-modern-food-lower-in-nutrients/4018578.article.

3. "What Vitamins You Should Take Is a Personalized Decision," Cleveland Clinic, March 20, 2024, https://health.cleveland-clinic.org/which-vitamins-should-you-take.

Tool 4.8:
Monitor Your Body

Regularly assess your physical and mental health.

Motivation

When you're not experiencing pain or other physical symptoms, it's easy to assume that your body is well. Even though you may feel fine, however, odds are that you may be functioning suboptimally in one or more ways. It's never been easier to measure potent biomarkers, either at home or by going to the lab. You can count your steps, check the quality of your sleep, and measure your calorie intake. These techniques can help you pinpoint the weaknesses in your health regime and determine what you need to change to reach your goals.

In a worst-case scenario, disease may be brewing beneath the surface. Unless you take proactive steps to investigate your health, you may be unaware of issues until they manifest at an advanced stage. Fortunately, personal fitness monitoring, especially combined with regular lab work and checkups with your doctor, can uncover latent conditions, enabling you to take action before they become serious.

Benefits

- Understand your body better and make informed choices.
- Discover issues before they become significant health problems.
- Gain a sense of control over your health.

Challenges

- The abundance of data can be overwhelming, and not all of it will be actionable.
- With work and home obligations, it may be hard to prioritize regular lab tests.

Application

At home, there are now numerous options for monitoring your health, many of them accessible through your phone or smartwatch. Some of the most common include tracking your heart rate, counting your steps, and measuring both the quantity and quality of your sleep.

These tools can be very useful for understanding and optimizing the functioning of your body. For example, if you discover that you aren't sleeping well, you can make changes to your sleep routine to encourage deeper rest. You may want to try wearing earplugs at night or changing your mattress. If you discover that you have a condition, such as sleep apnea, you can take steps to treat it. The variety of tools for health tracking is wide and constantly evolving, so it's best to do your own research online to discover what's currently available.

The next level of health monitoring involves visiting your doctor regularly—every three to six months. Depending on your age, stage of life, and general health indicators, your doctor may give you specific recommendations about staying healthy or improving your health, including getting lab work done. If your doctor doesn't request lab work, you should ask for it yourself.

Tests should include basic health markers such as your blood sugar and cholesterol count, vitamin and mineral levels, and other traditional health markers. In addition, you should ask for tests related to:

- **Sexually transmitted infections (STIs):** Even if you are married or otherwise in a monogamous relationship, it's worth getting tested occasionally.

- **Functional tests:** These include a thorough look at your nutrient levels, your diet, and the impact of any environmental toxins.

- **Genetic testing:** If you have a genetic predisposition to a particular disease, it's a good idea to get as much warning as possible so that you can take steps to limit your risk.

Most lab work should be done on an annual basis. If you see indications that something may be wrong, however, it's a good idea to ask your doctor for more frequent tests. Together, home monitoring and lab tests can alert you to potential problems or suboptimal performance as early as possible, giving you a chance to respond and, if necessary, change direction or seek treatment.

Further Reading

1. 23andMe genetic testing: https://23andme.com/.

2. Genetic Genie: https://geneticgenie.org/.

3. Kristin Samuelson, "Routine Medical Checkups Have Important Health Benefits," Northwestern Medicine News Center, June 11, 2021, https://news.feinberg.northwestern.edu/2021/06/11/routine-medical-checkups-have-important-health-benefits/.

4. Rajive Patel, "How Can We Self-Monitor Our Health?" Now-Patient, last updated July 16, 2024, https://nowpatient.com/blog/how-can-we-self-monitor-our-health.

Tool 4.9:
Agree to Be Hungry

Allowing ourselves to be hungry for a time can improve our relationship with food.

Motivation

Some people cannot bear the thought of being hungry, even for a little while. This creates an unhealthy relationship with food. They may begin planning their next meal well before they actually need to eat in order to eliminate the anxiety of feeling even a slight sensation of hunger.

The way you eat is probably still conditioned by habits you developed in childhood. Maybe you come from a household where you were told you had to finish everything on your plate at every meal. Alternatively, perhaps your parents said that you were eating too much and should lose weight. These messages, or other unhealthy experiences around food, may have caused you to want to eat more, even to the point of developing a food addiction!

Consciously listening to your body and agreeing to be hungry for a while can give you more control over your eating habits, allowing you to better meet your dietary goals. Additionally, there is some evidence to suggest that eating infrequently and allowing your stomach to empty between meals is healthy and helps digestion.

Benefits

- You learn to tune into your body's appetite signals.
- More agency over your eating choices.
- Better focus on your everyday activities.

Challenges

- Facing the fear of being hungry can be hard.
- Rewiring deeply ingrained habits takes willpower and persistence.

Application

This tool starts with making a choice to accept that there will be moments when you feel hungry. This starts with being present in your body, becoming aware of the sensation of hunger, and choosing to allow that sensation instead of following a pattern of eating the moment you feel hunger. This is an ongoing commitment to accepting hunger and being okay with not immediately satisfying the urge to eat. It's not a one-off choice.

The choice to look hunger in the eye can put you in a difficult emotional state, even to the point where you tell yourself that you are "starving" and that your survival depends on eating right away. You might even abhor hunger to the degree that you obsess about planning meals hours before you are actually hungry. If you find this tool challenging, remind yourself that you're not really going to perish if you are simply hungry for a short while.

Tool 4.10:
Stretching

Find opportunities in your day for a quick stretch.

Motivation

During the day, especially right after we awaken, many of us feel sluggish and sleepy. This effect can be compounded by poor sleep, injuries, and general stiffness or soreness. It's tempting to reach for a mug of coffee to provide a quick hit of energy, but stretching can also be an effective method of energizing ourselves whenever we start to sag.

Benefits

- Keeps your body flexible.
- Helps you feel more youthful.
- Supports joint and ligament health.

Challenges

- Performing stretches incorrectly can lead to discomfort, injury, or a lack of desired results.

Application

Habits usually stick most easily when we attach them to other habits (see Tool 1.17: Atomic Habits), so try to find something in your daily routine that triggers you to remember to stretch. This can be waking up, reaching your lunch break, or anything else that serves as a reminder.

If you have a dog or a cat, you'll see that they naturally stretch when they awaken and throughout the day, so it's clearly a natural tendency to elongate our limbs and breathe deeply. You don't need a lot of training to stretch—you can just raise your arms over your head, make a few arm circles, and touch your toes.

For a slightly more advanced routine, however, you can find dozens of videos on the web that provide inspiration and guidance. You may wish to allocate a specific amount of time, such as two, five, or ten minutes, and follow along with a favorite creator.

Whatever you choose, be gentle with yourself, particularly right after waking. The goal is to loosen up your body, get your blood flowing, and ease yourself into the day, not to perform complex yoga poses. Resist the inclination to do too much too fast, and check what feels right for you.

Tool 4.11:
Exercise Multiple Times a Week

Compound your benefits with more frequent sessions.

Motivation

Many of us find it difficult to exercise. It can be hard to start and often feels like torture until it ends. You might think that the solution is to do less and rest longer between workouts. While this can be true for people who are overtraining, there's a lot of value in sticking to a regular schedule. The less frequently we exercise, the more painful it feels and the tougher it is on the body. When we exercise often, however, our bodies release endorphins that make us feel good, motivating us to enjoy exercise and want to engage in it more.

Benefits

- As you work out more, you may start to enjoy it, motivating you to continue.
- You get better fitness and health results.

Challenges

- It may be hard to fit more sessions into your schedule.
- Breaking through the initial pain of unaccustomed exercise can be tough.

Application

If you only work out one or two times a week (or less), you may find it a struggle each time you decide to go to the gym or for a run. Adding in more sessions can help you move past this resistance by providing frequent reminders of why you choose to exercise, as well as more evidence of the benefits.

For best results, aim to put in at least three or four workout sessions each week, perhaps varying the type of activity to keep yourself engaged. You may be sore the day after you train and feel inclined to rest more, but as long as you haven't sustained an injury, muscular soreness is just the body's response to unaccustomed activity. It will soon adapt to an increased level of exercise.

To increase your desire to get off the couch and move, try finding a sport or game you enjoy (see Tool 4.2: Find Physical Activities You Enjoy). For a further motivational boost, you can hire a coach, join group sessions, or use an accountability buddy. Hopefully, with a little determination and support, you can quickly reach the point where extra sessions increase your morale rather than being a hurdle to overcome.

Further Reading

1. Mayo Clinic Staff, "Exercise: 7 Benefits of Regular Physical Activity," Mayo Clinic, August 25, 2023, https://mayoclinic. org/healthy-lifestyle/fitness/in-depth/exercise/art-20048389.

2. Mallory Creveling, "How Often Should You Work Out?" *Health*, last updated July 31, 2023, https://health.com/fitness/ how-many-days-work-out.

Tool 4.12:
Intermittent Fasting

Your eating schedule can significantly influence your health.

Motivation

One reason you may struggle to lose weight is the timing of your meals. There is promising evidence that fasting, especially at certain times of the day, is healthy and assists the body in burning fat, whereas eating at the wrong times can encourage the body to retain fat. You may find that restricting the hours during which you eat can boost your metabolism and help you lose weight more easily.

Benefits

- Has the potential to catalyze weight loss and improve body composition.
- Many people who fast report sleeping better and feeling more rested.
- Can reduce overall caloric intake.

Challenges

- Requires a lot of willpower at first as you get used to a new routine.
- Might conflict with the eating schedules of those close to you.

Application

The idea behind intermittent fasting is to give your body a window of time each day to eat and digest food and another window in which you avoid eating. Some people choose to eat during a six-hour window and fast the remaining eighteen hours, while others prefer an eight-hour or twelve-hour eating window, fasting for the rest of the day (these different styles are referred to as 6–18, 8–16, etc.). During the avoidance window, the goal is usually to resist consuming anything at all, not even a crumb, to keep the digestive system completely food-free. Adherents believe that this produces numerous benefits, such as increased autophagy, a process of cell renewal. However, if you can't or won't avoid eating completely for most of the day, that's okay—even reducing food intake for longer periods of time is beneficial.

If this approach seems a little too restrictive for you, you could try a lightweight version: Simply pick a period of time before bed—say three hours—and stop eating at the designated time. This can make it surprisingly easy to fast. For example, if you stop eating at 8 p.m., go to bed at 11 p.m., and eat breakfast at 8 a.m. the next morning, you will automatically fast for twelve hours.

Further Reading

1. "Intermittent Fasting: What is it, and how does it work?" Johns Hopkins Medicine, https://hopkinsmedicine.org/health/wellness-and-prevention/intermittent-fasting-what-is-it-and-how-does-it-work.

2. Kris Gunnars, "Intermittent Fasting 101—The Ultimate Beginner's Guide," Healthline, last updated May 3, 2024, https://healthline.com/nutrition/intermittent-fasting-guide#effects.

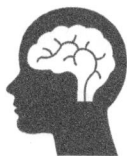

CHAPTER FIVE

MIND

"Knowing yourself is the beginning of all wisdom."

—Aristotle

The tools in this chapter are intended to help enhance your mind. One feature of a high-functioning mind is the capacity to store and access memories, so you'll discover tools to augment your natural recall, thus helping you remember what you've read, connect with people you've met, and understand why you want to remember these things in the first place.

But minds are more than simple memory receptors. Healthy minds think clearly and seek to understand the world in ways that lead to happier and fuller lives. To that end, there are tools here to assist you in questioning your belief systems and, just as importantly, the belief systems others may try to thrust on you. You will examine habitual thought patterns, learn to make new ones, and discover how to face your fears so you can prevent them from inhibiting you.

Another aspect of developing a resilient mind is taking care of it. That requires adequate sleep and giving your brain a chance to periodically empty itself, refresh, and recharge so that you are prepared to take on new thoughts. On top of all this, there are tools to support you in controlling your thoughts and retaining what you learn, beginning with writing book reviews, which can help you find clarity about what you've read and remember the information better.

Tool 5.1:
Write Book Reviews

Summarize books after reading them in order to better process and remember them.

Motivation

If you want to remember what you learned in a book, writing a book review is an excellent way to reinforce your memory. If you take just a few minutes to record what you have read after you finish a book, you will find you have a better understanding and recall of the material at a later date. You don't have to publish your review anywhere—the process is useful even if you don't. However, sending it to people or publishing it on social media or dedicated book review websites may benefit others. In turn, you can also learn something from your interactions with others about these reviews.

Benefits

- Summarizing challenges you to understand and articulate what you read.
- You gain a reference point you can use to jog your memory, even years later.
- Sharing what you read can be meaningful to you and others.

Challenges

- While writing reviews doesn't take long compared to reading the book, it can be challenging to prioritize finding even a few minutes for this endeavor.

Application

Shortly after you finish reading a book, take a few minutes to think over what you just read, then write a few paragraphs about what you recall. You can leaf through the book for additional information, but don't stress yourself out. You're not writing a book report for school. Note down what you want to remember—ideas that you'd like to reflect on, that you find meaningful, and that you believe will help you sometime in the future. The act of writing will help fix the information in your brain, enabling you to remember it more clearly. Also, the challenge of articulating your understanding of the book will help to solidify it.

There are many ways to write book reviews. You can use a notebook and pen, record audio files, or actually go online and review the book on book retailer sites or review sites. Each option will help you better understand the books you read and remember what you read.

Further Reading

Goodreads, a book review website: https://www.goodreads.com/.

Tool 5.2:
Own Your Echo Chamber

Recognize your default influences and make an effort to get out of the bubble they create.

Motivation

It's easy to get trapped in your own echo chamber and only surround yourself with people who think like you and consume similar media. If you succumb to this temptation, however, you will limit your ability to investigate your own bias. This will leave you at the mercy of the content you consume and the people who shape your opinions. At its most extreme, you may find yourself caught up in a belief system or a social circle that makes you blind to what's really happening in your world and unable to see your shackles.

Plato's Cave is a famous allegory depicting this state. A group of prisoners live chained in a cave, facing a blank wall. Objects passing behind them are projected onto the wall of the cave by a fire at the cave's entrance. The prisoners, unaware that what they see is but a pale shadow of life, name the shadows and believe them to be real. Owning your echo chamber is the equivalent of breaking out of the cave and investigating life as it is, not merely its reflection.

Benefits

- The ability to see all sides of a situation is a prerequisite to thinking critically and seeing often-hidden truths.
- Periodically challenging and updating your worldview is necessary for personal growth.

Challenges

- Admitting to uncertainty or a lack of knowledge can be frightening.
- Listening deeply to views we disagree with can feel like a waste of time and energy.

Application

When we've been exposed exclusively to particular patterns of thought, it's hard to see them as anything other than facts. If you grew up in a religious community, for example, you may believe the Bible is the literal truth without giving it a second thought. If you are a member of a pro-gun community, you will not hear a lot from those who wish to make it harder to own an assault rifle.

Many of us find it nearly impossible to challenge deeply ingrained beliefs on our own. Instead of exploring our own beliefs, we prefer to defend them with rhetoric. Straw man tactics, for example, purposely simplify or distort the views of others to misrepresent them and thus win the debate. We have a tendency to view our own arguments as soldiers in a war and feel compelled to defend them, even those that may be weak or unconvincing. If each argument is a soldier, then letting go of one is akin to stabbing a fellow soldier in the back on the field of battle. This approach blocks off the possibility of changing our minds and learning new truths.

If we wish to counter these tendencies, we need to become curious enough about alternatives to consciously expose ourselves to other viewpoints and, in doing so, empower our inner skeptic. One way to do this is to adopt the steel man approach. As the name suggests, the steel man is the opposite of the straw man. Instead of tearing down your opponent's argument, you bolster it to its strongest form before attacking it. Even if you don't agree with it fully, you may be able to discover some valuable insights this way.

To really get outside your echo chamber, you'll need to be open to the possibility that much of what you currently believe may be erroneous. If you're conservative, you may need to make an effort to read stories from the liberal media—and vice versa. Our natural biases may make it hard to do this, but they too should be challenged.

Exposing ourselves to many other points of view and other sources of news and information will help us to determine what is accurate and potentially break out of habits of thinking that are keeping us trapped. The ultimate point of this exercise isn't to prove ourselves right and others wrong but to discover the truth.

Further Reading

1. "Allegory of the Cave," Wikipedia, https://en.wikipedia.org/wiki/Allegory_of_the_cave.

2. "Straw Man," Wikipedia, https://en.wikipedia.org/wiki/Straw_man.

3. Will Bachman, "Steelmanning," Umbrex, https://umbrex.com/resources/tools-for-thinking/what-is-steelmanning/.

4. "Arguments as Soldiers," LessWrong (blog), https://lesswrong.com/tag/arguments-as-soldiers.

5. Tools for rational thinking and analyzing pseudoscience: https://rationalwiki.org/wiki/Main_Page.

Tool 5.3:
Be Curious

Get in touch with the desire to understand.

Motivation

When you're in an emotional situation and find yourself tempted to judge or criticize, reaching instead for curiosity can be an antidote to the negative relationship mechanics that often play out when judgment and criticism take over.

It's hard to be both judgemental *and* curious. Curiosity conveys an openness to understanding another person's perspective, whereas judgment comes from a fixed perception.

You may also experience curiosity when someone is telling you a story or explaining something to you. It's easy to squash that natural impulse, perhaps due to a fear of sounding stupid, but there's usually wisdom in the questions that arise in us. Tuning into your natural curiosity can be a powerful and beautiful tool for navigating the world.

Benefits

- Choosing curiosity over judgment or criticism can encourage others to open up to you.
- You will learn more about other people and the world through being curious.

Challenges

- You may need to overcome shyness, a fear of looking foolish, or concerns over wasting other people's time.
- Some people strongly believe they already know what they need to know and find it difficult to connect with their curiosity.

Application

It's important to practice genuine curiosity—asking questions from a place of truly wanting to understand. To do this, you will first need to tap into your natural curiosity. This is innate in all of us. Spend some time with a young child, and you will soon find yourself bombarded with questions as they explore the world, how it works, and why.

As adults, we may suppress our curiosity, perhaps feeling that we should know the answers to important questions by now or that it's inappropriate to interrupt the direction of a conversation by asking. We may be anxious about bothering others with our questions or unwilling to appear vulnerable in an emotionally charged conversation. To cover for our vulnerability, we may leap to criticism, which can feel easier than acknowledging that we don't fully understand the situation.

If we deny our curiosity, we will remain in the dark and may, in fact, make more blunders. We may mistake what someone needs to feel safe or misunderstand how to perform crucial tasks. It's important to understand, however, that there's a difference between asking from a genuine desire to understand and wrapping negative sentiments in questions to create a facsimile of curiosity. "What on earth is wrong with you?" is not an expression of genuine curiosity. A more productive approach might be to say, "Help me understand. Why did you behave that way?"

Further Reading

1. Leigh Spencer, "11 Benefits of Being Curious," Rest Less, January 19, 2023, https://restless.co.uk/health/healthy-mind/benefits-of-being-curious/.

2. Jonathan H. Westover, "Stay Curious: The Importance of Continually Asking Questions," *Forbes,* August 25, 2021, https://forbes.com/councils/forbescoachescouncil/2021/08/25/stay-curious-the-importance-of-continually-asking-questions/.

Tool 5.4:
Asking "Why"

Cultivate curiosity about the reason things happen.

Motivation

We all interpret the meaning of events, but unless we sincerely ask "why," we're bound to be blind to the circumstances leading to our present situation. At times, the reasons are obvious—you cut your finger, so you bandage it. Other actions stem from more complicated causes. Let's say the dry cleaner ruins your favorite shirt, and you threaten to sue them. Your unexpected rage, however, might not be purely about the shirt itself but more about the memories tied to the shirt, which belonged to your recently deceased best friend.

Asking "why" requires you to be curious (see Tool 5.3: Be Curious). Your brain is wired to explain everything that happens to you and to eliminate gaps in your understanding. When you encounter a situation, it immediately spits out a model of what has occurred, as well as how and why. Even though this model is by definition probabilistic, your lizard brain doesn't know this. It often clings to one option and sees it as objective reality.

By taking the time and energy to dig deeper and question your initial interpretations, you open yourself up to see a larger picture and consider options that would otherwise have been hidden from your sight.

Benefits

- By challenging our innate assumptions and continuously asking "why," we expand our knowledge and illuminate blind spots in our comprehension, fostering a deeper understanding of the world around us.

- This approach helps us better comprehend the perspectives of others, deepening our empathy and encouraging more meaningful, compassionate interactions.

- Asking "why" allows us to defuse conflict by breaking through negative cycles of assumption and blame.

Challenges

- Some assumptions and beliefs are so deeply embedded that it's hard to move beyond them.

- Sometimes, people may not be able to fully explain their actions, or their account may not seem entirely trustworthy or comprehensive, leaving you to wrestle with ambiguity.

- Use this tool judiciously—in certain contexts or cultures, asking "why" may appear intrusive or inappropriate.

Application

The first step to a better understanding of a person's motives is relaxing the assumption that you already know them or that it's ever possible to know them for sure. When confronted with a situation that you don't fully understand, take a moment to pause and ask why things are the way they are. If you are engaged in an argument, for example, instead of responding based on your immediate assumptions or beliefs about the other person's behavior, pose a question—ask them why they chose to act or speak as they did. This response allows you to step back from your preconceptions and approach the situation with an empathetic and curious mindset, which can lead to a more nuanced understanding and foster effective communication.

If someone appears upset or angry with you, resist the urge to become defensive. Instead, gently ask them why they feel the way they do. This approach has two key benefits: It defuses the immediate tension and also provides valuable insight into the other person's perspective, facilitating a more constructive path through the conflict.

As Socrates wisely said, "The only true wisdom is in knowing you know nothing." This is not to encourage self-deprecation but to serve as a reminder to remain humble in our pursuit of understanding. When we question our assumptions and seek the "why," we acknowledge the limitations of our knowledge and open ourselves to continuous learning. This humble curiosity paves the way to deeper wisdom and insight, and it all begins by asking "why."

When asking "why," remember to adopt an attitude of curiosity, not aggression. You're not asking people to justify their actions; you're seeking greater understanding of their behavior. Ask "why" as a means to encourage dialogue, enhance understanding, and nurture empathy.

Further Reading

1. In the workplace: Kameshia L. Freeman, "The Importance of Asking Why," LinkedIn, March 22, 2022, https://linkedin.com/pulse/importance-asking-why-kameshia-l-freeman/.

2. In relationships: Marty Nemko, "The Importance of Asking Why," Psychology Today, February 13, 2022, https://psychologytoday.com/us/blog/how-do-life/202202/the-importance-asking-why.

3. Leigh Spencer, "11 Benefits of Being Curious," Rest Less, January 19, 2023, https://restless.co.uk/health/healthy-mind/benefits-of-being-curious/.

4. Karen Maeyens, "The Value of Asking Questions," TEDx Talks, November 2017, https://ted.com/talks/karen_maeyens_the_value_of_asking_questions.

Tool 5.5:
Morning Pages

Every morning, fill a few pages with stream-of-consciousness writing.

Motivation

The concept of morning pages originates from *The Artist's Way* by Julia Cameron. Cameron proposed the practice as a way to clear out blocked emotions and free up creativity. Even if you don't consider yourself an artist, producing morning pages has numerous benefits. It can help you relax, find mental clarity, and live with more creativity and energy in every area of your life.

Sometimes, when you get stressed or tense, you may find it hard to discipline and focus your mind. Without an outlet for the tension, you bear the mental and emotional cost of these feelings. You risk taking out your negative emotions on other people or becoming distracted and finding it hard to complete important tasks. By dumping the contents of your brain onto paper, you can process your emotions and find a private outlet for them. This can lessen their intensity and free up mental space, better equipping you to meet the day.

Benefits

- Helps you process your emotions.
- Can increase motivation and joy.
- Reconnects you with the source of your creativity.

Challenges

- Forcing yourself to write when uninspired can be awkward.
- You may find yourself overthinking instead of just writing what comes to mind.

Application

When you first wake up in the morning, before you dive into your day, start writing. For many reasons, Cameron advocates writing by hand as opposed to typing. For example, she believes that the slower pace generates a deeper, more mindful approach, along with a more tactile experience. If you feel more comfortable using a computer, however, that still conveys many benefits. In any case, make sure you shield yourself from distractions, digital or otherwise (see Tool 1.3: Disconnect).

Regardless of the medium, start writing. You can set a goal to fill a particular number of pages (Cameron recommends three) or set a timer and write until it expires. Try to capture your initial, raw thoughts and resist the temptation to edit yourself, even if you find yourself thinking thoughts that feel unexpected or scary. Also, don't worry about grammar or spelling. This is your private space, and nobody is here to judge or criticize you.

The purpose of using the Morning Pages tool is to foster your creativity and process mental obstacles by engaging with your thoughts and emotions. The key is to stay consistent, remain open to what comes up, and give yourself the space to explore your inner world.

Further Reading

1. Julia Cameron, *The Artist's Way: A Spiritual Path to Higher Creativity* (TarcherPerigee, 2016).

2. "Journaling Techniques: 12 Tips for Writing Morning Pages," MasterClass, last updated August 23, 2021, https://masterclass.com/articles/tips-for-writing-morning-journal-pages.

Tool 5.6:
Physical Memory Tricks

Use objects and your body as reminders.

Motivation

Memory objects are useful reminders to your future self of something related to a physical location. While digital reminders exist, they are limited because in some situations, you may not be able to check your phone, or by the time you do, it's too late. A classic example is remembering to do something or take something with you as you leave the house. Often, a strategically placed unique object that catches your eye is the best reminder.

Similarly, you've probably been in a situation where you're having a conversation and something you want to remember crosses your mind. One way to handle this is to write yourself a note (see "Capture" in Tool 1.7: Getting Things Done). However, you may not have a notepad available, or it might not be appropriate to use one during the conversation. A tool you can use in this situation is to simply cross your fingers and keep them crossed until the conversation is over. This will remind you that you had something important on your mind.

Benefits

- Offloading the task of recalling something to physical objects frees up your mind.
- You can use a variety of objects and methods according to the situation.
- Your fingers are always available for crossing, no matter where you are.

Challenges

- If someone moves your object, you might miss the reminder.
- If you have to maintain crossed fingers for a long time, it can get uncomfortable and even painful.

Application

Here are a few things you can try, depending on the situation.

If you want to remember to take something with you when you leave for work, the simplest way is often to place that object by the door in a way that you can't miss when you walk out. It's best if the object physically obstructs your path. However, that's not mandatory. If you can't do this (e.g., for fear of small kids moving or damaging the object), you can place a secondary memory object in a visible place to remind you to take the first one.

Sticky notes can also serve as useful ad hoc reminders. Advanced users of this tool might even purchase some colored Plasticine to serve as memory objects, which can be shaped in various ways for different purposes.

Crossing your fingers to remember is as easy as it sounds. Simply cross two fingers and keep them crossed until you are done with the conversation. When you get a spare moment and notice that your fingers are crossed, this will trigger you to remember and note down your original thought. If you find that your fingers uncross without you noticing, try tightening up your fingers and solidifying your awareness.

Tool 5.7:
Follow Up After Meeting New People

**After meeting someone new,
bolster the connection with a message.**

Motivation

If you have an active social or business life, you frequently meet new people you would like to see again, whether at parties, networking events, conferences, or in other circumstances. Even if you don't yet have a specific plan in mind, you know that you would like to maintain and develop some sort of connection with them. One way to encourage a connection is to send them a quick message after the meeting, recapping your impressions from the encounter.

Benefits

- Reaching out to people serves to anchor the meeting in both your memories, even if it's a while before you correspond further.
- It creates an immediate opportunity to delve deeper if you're so inclined.
- In cases where you don't speak again for some time, you'll be able to refer back to this summary of your encounter, which can jog your memory.

Challenges

- If you're not planning to immediately pursue further connection, it can feel weird to send a recap, especially in non-business contexts.

Application

The simplest version of this tool is to reflect on social or business events, perhaps the morning after you attend or during a weekly review. Consider whether you've met anyone who piqued your interest and with whom you'd like to connect further. If so, and if you don't already have their contact details, try to find a way of getting in touch, perhaps via social networks or mutual friends. Then, write them a simple message, expressing appreciation for meeting them and possibly mentioning one or two topics you enjoyed discussing with them.

To take this tool to the next level, you can come to events prepared. Collect business cards, ask for people's last names and/or phone numbers, and even jot down brief summaries of what you talked about. Afterward, when you get a moment, these records will help you craft your outreach for maximum value and greatly streamline the process.

In order to circumvent some of the awkwardness of reaching out to someone you don't know well, you may wish to be transparent. Let them know that you enjoyed their company and that you aren't necessarily looking for an immediate follow-up or approaching them with a specific agenda, but rather that you are interested in staying in touch and seeing how the connection evolves.

Further Reading

1. Indeed Editorial Team, "How to Write a Networking Follow-Up Email (Plus 5 Samples)," Indeed, last updated August 15, 2024, https://indeed.com/career-advice/career-development/networking-follow-up-email.

2. "Memorandum of Conversation," Wikipedia, https://en.wikipedia.org/wiki/Memorandum_of_conversation.

3. Larry Sharpe, "How to Follow Up After a Networking Event," LinkedIn, December 17, 2024, https://linkedin.com/pulse/how-follow-up-after-networking-larry-sharpe/.

Tool 5.8:
Silent Date

Spend quiet time with someone you care about.

Motivation

There are times when you may want to spend time with your partner but, for one reason or another, you don't want to make conversation. Perhaps you've had an argument and the atmosphere between you is tense. Perhaps you haven't seen each other for a while and you want to reconnect slowly. Perhaps you're both stressed and exhausted and you crave the comfort of one another's presence without the effort of communicating.

The motivation can be positive as well as negative. Maybe you're both introverted people, and explicit permission to be silent helps you feel closer. Maybe removing the distraction of words allows you to see one another more clearly. Maybe you enjoy the experience of flirting in silence, using gestures and body language. Whatever your reasons, a silent date differs from simply hanging out without speaking. It's a mutually agreed-upon commitment to refrain from speaking.

Benefits

- If emotions are running high, agreeing not to speak can sometimes soothe the situation and allow you to feel closer.
- Being with someone you know well in silence can give you a whole new perspective on who they are.

Challenges

- It can be tempting to break the silence. At times, this may be appropriate, but it can be hard to set guidelines beforehand.

- There's a risk that your mood (or your partner's) could shift toward coldness or resentment as opposed to warmth.

Application

This tool is similar to some experiences at mindfulness retreats (see Tool 6.3: Go On a Retreat). You can turn it into a meditation, although that's not essential. The fundamental idea is simple: You make an agreement with another person to be silent for a particular amount of time.

There are almost no limits to the ways you can apply this tool. You may choose to partake in activities together or do different activities in the same room simultaneously. You can even sit silently at separate laptops, both working on projects. You can face one another and look into each other's eyes or curl up on the couch and cuddle. You can share a meal in contemplative silence. You can watch TV, dance to music, or listen to a podcast. Whatever you choose, try to remain mindful of and connected to the other person as opposed to slipping into self-distraction.

It's a good idea to anticipate situations that might require you to speak and create some guidelines before entering into silence. For example, you may want to allow technical talk, such as "I need to use the bathroom," or employ a safe word in case the emotional experience becomes overwhelming.

Further Reading

1. Léa Rose Emery, "Why Moments of Silence Are Great for Your Relationship," *Brides,* last updated December 1, 2022, https://brides.com/story/why-silence-is-great-for-your-relationship.

Tool 5.9:
Find Your Purpose

Actively seek your life's true north.

Motivation

In the midst of our everyday lives and responsibilities, it's all too easy to get mired in busy work and lose sight of what's important to us. After living like a hamster on a wheel for a while, we begin to feel empty or directionless. We may be unsure what to do with our lives or struggle to feel a sense of meaning.

In such times, actively working to define your purpose can help. This is an ongoing process. Many people believe that, when they seek greater meaning in life, they must find their one true purpose, which encompasses everything they are and will ever want to be and do. Or, they decide that this problem is so intractable that they should give up and only aim for short-term goals. The truth lies in the middle ground. It's possible to find a purpose, live by it, and adapt it as your life progresses.

Benefits

- With a clear purpose as your compass, daily decisions become easier.
- Can instill a powerful sense of meaning.
- Can nourish your motivation, especially in difficult times.

Challenges

- Articulating a direction for your entire life can feel daunting.
- It's often hard to know the first step in discovering and refining your purpose.

Application

There are a lot of ways to discover a sense of purpose. For example, you can participate in workshops designed to help attendees connect with their purpose, work with a coach who specializes in this field, or explore writing exercises. One good exercise is to connect with and list your values, then attempt to articulate the world you're seeking to create and how. Be specific. Try to express this in a sentence using this format:

I create a world of _____ by _____.

Examples of purposes can be:

- I create a world of radical acceptance by accepting myself, others, and what I can't change.
- I create a world of beauty and creativity by removing boundaries to free expression.

Alternatively, you can adapt this format to articulate more specific goals. For example:

- I reduce class inequality in South Africa by building an inclusive business.
- I make sure my family stays loving and connected by creating opportunities to spend quality time together.

The scope and content is really up to you. However, using the present tense can feel more actionable and concrete.

Another compass you can use to orient yourself toward your purpose is the Zuzunaga Venn Diagram of Purpose, often misrepresented as the Japanese concept of *ikigai*, a reason for living. According to Zuzunaga, the center of this diagram is the place where various phenomena overlap:

- What the world needs

- What you are good at doing
- What you can get paid to do
- What you love doing

Zuzunaga Venn Diagram of Purpose

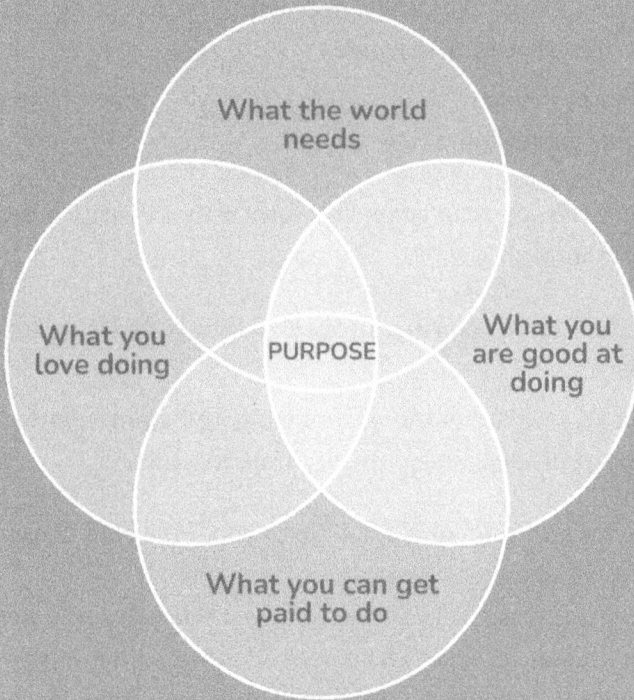

What the world needs

What you love doing

PURPOSE

What you are good at doing

What you can get paid to do

Tool 5.10:
Sleep Hygiene

Invest in the quantity and quality of your sleep.

Motivation

Sometimes, it seems as though modern life conspires against allowing us enough sleep. Our jobs are stressful; we live in urban areas filled with noise and distraction; and electronic devices, especially social networking apps, hijack our brains, keeping us hooked on dopamine when we want to drift off.

Unless we take conscious steps to protect our sleeping environment, we are likely to suffer from shorter-duration, lower-quality sleep. This affects every aspect of our lives, from our health to our relationships to our ability to focus. Sleep hygiene refers to any strategies that enable us to sleep more deeply, restfully, and consistently.

Benefits

- Better quality of sleep improves all aspects of your life—physical, mental, and emotional.

Challenges

- When you're overstimulated, you may be reluctant to wind down and feel an urge to continue engaging with the world.

Application

General trends indicate that not only are most of us sleeping less but also the quality of our sleep is declining. This makes us all more tired and, therefore, less effective, productive, and happy during our waking hours. The most pervasive cause of poor sleep hygiene is electronic devices. When we're wired from excessive screen time, we find it difficult to calm down and sleep. Our electronics bombard us with blue light wavelengths, which increase wakefulness and can disrupt healthy sleep patterns. Aside from blue light, phone notifications also trigger excessive adrenaline. Apps are designed to stimulate the brain's reward mechanism and keep us swiping, scrolling, or messaging. That rush makes it difficult to go to sleep.

Therefore, controlling your access to electronic devices is one way to improve your chances of falling asleep quickly and getting good quality sleep. Generally speaking, it's beneficial to your focus to disable many of these notifications, and you can even configure your phone to block some apps completely as you approach bedtime. Many modern phones also have a setting that allows you to turn off blue light emissions in the evening. Ideally, it's best to stay away from all electronics for two to three hours before you go to bed. And if you truly want a good night's sleep, do not watch the news or anything stimulating before tucking in.

Additionally, there are several other habits you can get into to create a restful bedroom environment and nurture better sleep. Keep your bedroom very dark and as quiet as possible, with little external stimulation. The human body sleeps best in cool temperatures, so you may want to invest in a fan or air conditioning if you live in a hot climate. Keep your bedtime and your pre-bed routine consistent so that you send signals to your brain that it's time to wind down and prepare for sleep. Additionally, try to avoid eating close to bedtime; the digestive process can prevent you from fully relaxing.

If your mind still races after all this, you can try taking a hot shower before bed, applying calming essential oils to your pillow, or—if you regularly struggle with insomnia—seeking professional help from a sleep specialist.

Further Reading

1. Rudy Mawer, "Top 15 Proven Tips to Sleep Better at Night," Healthline, last updated May 29, 2024, https://healthline.com/nutrition/17-tips-to-sleep-better.

2. Rob Newsom, "Blue Light: What It Is and How It Affects Sleep," SleepFoundation, last updated January 12, 2024, https://sleepfoundation.org/bedroom-environment/blue-light.

Tool 5.11:
Face Your Fear

Stand up to the things that scare you.

Motivation

Fear can distort our perceptions, making threats appear larger than they are. When we run from our fears, they grow, potentially overwhelming us. Only when we stand up to the things that scare us can we determine how great the dangers really are and respond accordingly.

At times, these fears may be relatively frivolous, such as a fear of heights that prevents us from going bungee jumping. On occasions when we do face something truly terrifying, however, such as a potentially fatal disease, overcoming our fear will enable us to make better decisions, such as choosing the right treatment options and sharing profound moments with family and friends.

Benefits

- Fear often masks important truths.
- When we confront what scares us, we grow emotionally and become more resilient.

Challenges

- Fear can be very convincing, and it's difficult to separate legitimate warnings from false caution.

Application

One way to think of fear is through this acronym: "False evidence appears real." In many cases, fear is the creation of our minds and bears little resemblance to the actual dangers of a situation.

A powerful way to challenge this false evidence is to present your mind with new evidence that counteracts it. This is the same principle parents use to convince their children there isn't a monster in the cupboard or under the bed. When they turn on the lights or shine a flashlight into the shadows, they demonstrate that the fear isn't matched by reality.

You can do something similar to short-circuit many fears you encounter as an adult. Research your fear until you have a realistic perspective on it. This can help with phobias such as a fear of flying. Flying is an extremely safe method of travel, much safer than driving, yet many people feel nervous on airplanes. Putting the risks into context can be reassuring.

Another option is exposure therapy, which requires gradually more intense encounters with whatever you're afraid of until you become more comfortable. If you're frightened of spiders, for example, you start by looking at a picture of a spider. As the fear dissipates, you progress to sitting in close proximity to live spiders and maybe even allowing them to walk across your hand until you become more comfortable in their presence. This is not to say that your fears are always unwarranted. Some spiders are dangerous and deserve a wide berth.

A third technique is to employ a mantra, such as the Litany Against Fear popularized by the classic sci-fi novel *Dune*. In the novel, people seeking to focus their minds during crises repeat this litany, which goes like this:

"I must not fear.

Fear is the mind-killer.

Fear is the little-death that brings total obliteration.

I will face my fear."[8]

Further Reading

1. "Facing Your Fears," Better Health, https://nhs.uk/every-mind-matters/mental-wellbeing-tips/self-help-cbt-techniques/facing-your-fears/.

---

[8] Frank Herbert, *Dune* (Ace, 1990).

Tool 5.12:
Short-Circuit Habits

**Learn to break away from automated habits and
gain control over your actions.**

Motivation

We all do certain things automatically, from brushing our teeth, to driving to work, to switching on the TV. Some habits are healthy; they keep us gainfully employed, physically in shape, or in fully-functioning relationships. These are excellent automated habits to maintain. Sometimes, however, we reflexively do things without thinking them through—to our detriment.

When we regularly indulge in unhealthy habits, we often find that we're not living in accordance with our values and damage our well-being. Succumbing to poor habits can make us feel like we have little choice in the world and are not living with intention, whereas challenging them can give us back our sense of agency.

Benefits

- Break bad habits and stop indulging in behaviors that are not good for you.
- Live more authentically by making choices aligned with who you really are.

Challenges

- If the habits are truly ingrained in your mind, this can be very hard.
- Merely altering your habits without digging deeper into their emotional roots can lead to internal conflict.

Application

The first step is to identify the habits you want to address. You can do this by listing them on paper or digitally or by simply by taking a mental inventory. Once you've done this, be on the lookout for moments when one of them takes over and dictates your behavior.

When you're about to do something you'd like more control over, stop, take a couple of long breaths, and ask yourself why you are about to do whatever it is. Try to connect with your authentic self, deep inside you, and truly understand what is calling you to engage in the behavior. What needs are you fulfilling?

At times, you may discover that the answer feels right, positive, and healthy. In this case, you should go ahead and act on the impulse. Otherwise, you should exercise self-control and do something else instead.

Let's say you see a delicious-looking cake, and your knee-jerk reaction is to eat it. If you are on a diet or trying to cut back on sugar, however, stop for a moment and think about the cake. Do you really want it, or are you reaching for it out of habit? Are you hungry? What emotions are present? If you really want it, go ahead and enjoy it. If you're just reaching for it because it's in front of you and you habitually eat tempting food when it's available, you can choose to hold firm and find another option, like eating something nourishing or going for a walk.

Further Reading

1. Tool 5.13: Allow Yourself to Be Bored
2. Charles Duhigg, *The Power of Habit: Why We Do What We Do in Life and Business* (Random House, 2014).

Tool 5.13:
Allow Yourself to Be Bored

Occasional boredom is healthy, not something we need to fix.

Motivation

When we catch ourselves feeling bored, it's easy to conclude that we are doing something wrong and immediately alter our behavior. We may decide that we should work more, get some exercise, or put together a grocery list. Alternatively, we may feel a powerful urge to scroll through social media or slump in front of the TV. Another way to look at boredom, however, is that it may be an indication that we are not fully present. If we refrain from attempting to fix our boredom and instead observe it, we can learn the lessons it has to teach us.

Pauses like this can bring us into dialogue with a deeper layer of truth where we can witness our unexamined habits (see Tool 5.12: Short-Circuit Habits). This tool starts by investigating our boredom and discovering what's possible when we allow it.

When boredom hits, we may turn to our old habits to distract ourselves even before we've had a chance to consciously choose what we're doing. By getting in touch with our boredom, we can uncover the root causes of our dissatisfaction and defeat the temptation to indulge in habits that don't serve us.

Benefits

- Allows us to peek at the knowledge that lies hidden beneath boredom.
- More control over our choices and behaviors.
- Awareness can bring a sense of pleasure that doesn't depend on external stimuli.

Challenges

- Sitting quietly with boredom instead of masking it may feel increasingly unpleasant.
- Ingrained habits may maintain a powerful draw, making it very tempting to succumb to them instead of exploring the emotions they mask.

Application

When you catch yourself doing something automatically or engaging in a habit that you're not sure serves you, this might be a sign you are bored. Try to resist the temptation to be active with no purpose and lean into your present experience.

Pausing for a moment and becoming aware of your boredom invites you to explore the present moment. How is your body? Are you well rested? Aside from boredom, what other emotions are present? What do you need right now other than a momentary distraction?

Sometimes, this type of inquiry will bring valuable insights into your life, habits, and choices. These insights may allow you to identify patterns, break unconscious habits, and create actionable changes. Over time, these subtle shifts may build into significantly different choices.

To take this tool further, spend a little time making an inventory of your negative habits, such as emotional eating or reflexively scrolling through your phone. Most of us scan social media, check our email, or shop online more often than we really need to. These activities give us a quick dopamine hit but don't satisfy our deeper needs.

Once you understand your go-to solutions to boredom, you can investigate these habits. Do you really need to pick up your phone, or would you rather do something else—perhaps nothing at all?

Further Reading

1. Jamie Ducharme, "Being Bored Can Be Good for You—If You Do It Right. Here's How," *Time*, January 4, 2019, https://time.com/5480002/benefits-of-boredom/.

2. Shane W. Bench and Heather C. Lench, "On the Function of Boredom," *Behavioral Sciences* 3, no. 3: (August 15, 2013), https://www.mdpi.com/2076-328X/3/3/459.

CHAPTER SIX

SPIRIT

"The longest journey is the journey inward."

—Dag Hammarskjöld

This final chapter contains a collection of tools for awakening to your life purpose and finding self-acceptance. They will help you make peace with the fact that life always contains some kind of discomfort, and therefore you will never feel 100 percent complete.

We encounter various situations and mental states from extreme hardship to total ecstasy. The way we relate to these varied scenarios can have a subtle yet significant impact on our lived experiences and senses of well-being. At one end of the spectrum, if we resist what life brings us, even small annoyances can feel intensely unpleasant, leading us to experience life's inevitable bumps as suffering. Alternatively, if we learn to fully accept the reality of the present moment, we can alleviate and potentially transcend physical and emotional pain, perhaps even reaching a transcendent states of mind.

There are many reasons why we may take an interest in spiritual topics. Some of us come to spirituality after attaining material goals and finding our success unfulfilling. Others feel a nagging sense that there must be something more beyond the mundane world or seek a deeper meaning in everyday activities. Whatever our motivation, the tools in this chapter offer pathways to explore.

This, however, leads us into one of the trickiest conundrums encountered by spiritual seekers: The goal-oriented mind may latch onto the prospect of winning the spiritual game for example by getting to heaven or becoming Enlightened, which can entrench suffering rather than alleviating it. Some of the tools in this chapter (for example, Tool 6.7: Enlightenment Is Always Now and Tool 6.8: Beware of Spiritual Ego) address this experience.

Perhaps it's natural that the Pillar Tool in this chapter is Meditation, a unique approach to becoming present, quieting the mind, and exploring your mind and reality firsthand. Meditation, however, is not the only path to spiritual awareness. You will also find other tools that help you question and feel comfortable with your place in the universe and with your suffering, along with tools to help you discern what you can and cannot change about your life.

Although this chapter does touch on the concept of God, utilizing these tools does not depend on any specific religious perspective. They can be useful to atheists, along with people of all religions. Unlike the tools you'll find in other chapters, many of those you'll find here are intended to spark self-reflection and perhaps a new perspective on life as opposed to generating practical, technical applications. Let's take a breath, clear the mind, and explore what the tools have to offer.

Tool 6.1:
𝕀 Meditation

Practice paying attention to what is happening right now.

Motivation

These days, meditation is gaining mainstream popularity, from dozens of meditation apps to the Netflix show *Headspace Guide to Meditation*, as well as through tens of thousands of academic papers on meditation. Meditation can reduce stress, provide health benefits, and help you be more aware and in control.

Meditation lets you observe your thought patterns and emotions in real time, reduce reactive responses, and change your behavior. Finally, perhaps the ultimate benefit of meditation is that it can be a path to liberate you from ego delusion—the idea that there exists a "you" that's separate from the world and is subjectively more important than everything else.

Benefits

- Helps you feel calm and centered throughout the day.
- Allows you to observe your thoughts and feelings and decide how to act on them.
- Helps you gain insight into your thought patterns and the nature of consciousness.

Challenges

- Many people feel that they do not have time to meditate.
- People believe that they should succeed in meditation and may become frustrated when they feel that they're failing.
- It can be hard to sit still for longer than a few minutes.

Application

There are multiple ways to meditate, including mindfulness meditation, body scans, walking meditation, OSHO Dynamic Meditation, nondual meditations, and more. You can meditate with your eyes open or closed, in silence or guided, and even while engaged in other activities, like doing the dishes or conversing with people. The ultimate benefits of meditation are realized when it's not done as a separate practice but rather integrated into your everyday life.

One of the most common forms of meditation is mindfulness. To practice mindfulness meditation, start by setting aside some time. Ten or twenty minutes is fine, but if you're low on time, even five minutes can be beneficial. Sit with your eyes closed and observe what is happening moment by moment. Your objective is simply to notice everything that happens—thoughts, feelings, physical sensations, and sounds—without judgment and without holding on to anything that catches your attention.

You're not trying *not* to think but rather to just notice your thoughts and other phenomena such as feelings and sensations. If you catch yourself lost in thought, gently return to the practice of observation. And if you find that you're judging yourself as "not meditating well enough," simply observe that as another occurrence. It might be easiest, especially in the beginning, to meditate using a recorded guide or an app or even to attend live meditation sessions.

Attention is like a muscle, which meditation builds. The best way to build and maintain that muscle is with daily practice. Even a short meditation, repeated daily, is better than a long but sporadic one. As mentioned above, there are various ways to meditate, each with unique characteristics. While it's good to have a core practice you can rely on, it's also worthwhile to experiment and find what attracts you at any particular time (see Tools 6.2: Everyday Mindfulness and 6.3: Go On a Retreat for a few suggestions). Whatever you choose, try not to restrict your practice to formal sessions; this tool is meant to be integrated via short yet meaningful mindfulness moments throughout your day.

Remember, meditation is a lifelong practice; it's not something you achieve and forget about. There are always higher levels of awareness to be reached in the present moment.

Further Reading

1. Michael Taft, *The Mindful Geek: Secular Meditation for Smart Skeptics* (Cephalopod Rex, 2015).

2. Sam Harris, *Waking Up: A Guide to Spirituality Without Religion* (Simon & Schuster, 2015).

3. Sam Harris's app, Waking Up: https://wakingup.com/.

Tool 6.2:
Everyday Mindfulness

Extend your awareness practice beyond the meditation cushion.

Motivation

Meditation doesn't have to be done sitting still with your eyes closed in a silent room. The goal of practicing is to be more aware in your daily life. To this end, bringing a meditative mindset to a variety of situations can be helpful. Sometimes, you can add more mindful minutes to your day by splicing meditation into activities you are already doing, like walking, eating, or even doing the dishes.

Benefits

- When meditating, you can also enjoy your usual activities, such as walking, dancing, and eating, at the same time.
- An open, nonjudgmental state can enrich your daily experience.
- Practicing meditation in a range of contexts sharpens your ability to remain mindful in more challenging scenarios.

Challenges

- Practicing in stimulus-rich environments can be more distracting than sitting peacefully in a quiet room.
- Meditating during an activity can feel like an extra mental effort, which you might not always be up for.

Application

An easy first step could be to explore meditating in your usual seated position but keep your eyes open instead of closing them. This technique exposes you to the outside world while still in a meditative context and lets you experiment with keeping your focus in the face of external stimuli. You can also try meditating in a noisy location, such as on a bench on the street. Whatever the scenario, the practice remains the same: Notice whatever is happening inside or outside your body and return your attention to your chosen object of meditation, such as your breath or sensations in your body.

If you enjoy going for walks, try walking meditation. You can set a timer or just walk a predetermined route. Paying attention to your pattern of footsteps can be a useful anchor here. To start with, choosing a less-traveled path, perhaps in nature, can be easier than walking busy city streets. Another thing you can do is pick a meal and eat it quietly, without scrolling through your phone. Just focus on immersing yourself in the tastes, smells, and textures of the food. This idea can also make for an interesting mindful date night.

Another option is dancing meditation. There are many different types: OSHO Dynamic Meditation is a five-step structured progression, with different energies and guidance for each step. There are also unstructured mindful dancing events where you can move as you wish. You can even play a few songs in the privacy of your home and shake your body while keeping your awareness engaged.

You can do all these activities silently or while listening to guided meditations—whichever you prefer. In addition to these types of mindful activities, you might want to try turning transitions from one activity to the next into an opportunity for a few mindful moments. Some apps, such as Waking Up, include a "Moments" feature designed to help you catch such transitions. You can also program your phone or watch to vibrate at random intervals as a reminder to be aware.

Further Reading

1. "Dynamic Meditation," Wikipedia, https://en.wikipedia.org/wiki/Dynamic_meditation.
2. Waking Up app: https://wakingup.com/.

Tool 6.3:
Go On a Retreat

Schedule concentrated time to relax, reflect, and meditate.

Motivation

When you want to accelerate your personal development or work on an issue intensively, a retreat can be very helpful. In an environment where everything is set up to support your progress, including professional guidance from skilled and compassionate facilitators, you can rapidly achieve results that would otherwise take a long time.

If there's something you want to devote some immersive time to working on, or if you feel that your growth in a certain area is stagnating, you may want to schedule a retreat to give it your full focus.

Benefits

- Can provide a significant boost to your personal development or therapeutic processes.
- At many retreats, you avoid using your phone, which creates a rare and valuable opportunity for self-focus.
- Freedom from the responsibility of choosing what to do with your time can be quite liberating.

Challenges

- Disconnecting from daily life and committing to one thing for significant periods can feel daunting.
- Some retreats—particularly psychedelic or sexuality retreats—require a high level of trust in leaders and facilitators.

Application

First, it's important to determine what you're looking for in a retreat. There are seemingly infinite types of retreats available, so think carefully. Do you want to practice meditation? Deepen your therapeutic journey? Explore the world of psychedelics? Something else?

Next, find a facilitator or organization you like. Seek out recommendations or read their websites to get a feeling for their style and whether it's a match for you. Do your due diligence by talking to people who have attended the retreats you're interested in or by reading reviews online to ensure they are reputable. Any retreat requires you to trust the organizers, some more than others. If you fly to Peru for an ayahuasca retreat, for example, you will ingest mind-altering substances and put yourself in a vulnerable state.

You should also consider your schedule and budget. When do you want to travel, and how can you handle the logistics as seamlessly as possible? How much are you willing to invest in your retreat?

It would be impossible to detail every option in this book, but here are a few possibilities you may want to explore:

- **Therapeutic retreats such as an inner child retreat:** These retreats are about connecting with your younger self, talking to your parents in your mind's eye, or taking a different perspective in order to repair what was broken in your childhood or fix damage from trauma.

- **Silent or Vipassana retreats:** On a Vipassana meditation retreat, you will spend several days in silence, practicing meditation in many contexts (sitting, walking, eating, etc.). Instead of speech, you will focus on sharpening your awareness of your mind and body.

- **Psychedelic retreats:** There are numerous substances believed to open the mind, access non-mundane states of consciousness, and generate life-changing insights. Ayahuasca is the most common, but others include DMT, psilocybin, and MDMA.

- **Sexuality retreats, including Tantric and other practices:** Sexuality retreats come in various forms, ranging in spiciness from mild to extreme. Some are for individuals, others are for monogamous couples, and others are for open couples. If attending with a partner, it's essential to discuss boundaries beforehand so you both have a positive experience. Remember, you are in control and don't need to do anything you feel uncomfortable with.

- **Yoga retreats:** If you have an existing yoga practice, a dedicated retreat can be an opportunity to deepen it, explore the philosophical aspects that are often missing from shorter classes, and connect with a community of like-minded people.

Further Reading

1. William Hart, *The Art of Living: Vipassana Meditation* (HarperOne, 2009).

2. Michaela Trimble, "Psychedelic Travel Experiences Are More Popular Than Ever," *Condé Nast* Traveler, April 17, 2024, https://cntraveler.com/story/psychedelic-travel-experiences.

3. Sarah Barrell, "The Rise of Wellness Travel, from Rewilding to Yoga and Pilgrimages," *National Geographic,* July 28, 2023, https://nationalgeographic.com/travel/article/wellness-travel-rewilding-yoga-pilgrimages.

Tool 6.4:
Kōans and Mu

There is value in exercising the mind with impossible questions.

Motivation

Zen *kōans* are stories, statements, or questions for which a solution is sought but no such solution or answer exists. For example:

- If a tree falls in the forest and nobody is there, does it make a sound?
- Does a dog have Buddha-nature?
- Show me your original face before you were born.

Such propositions defy our usual way of thinking, and any attempt to arrive at a definitive answer can be daunting or impossible. Nonetheless, there is value in asking them repeatedly and observing what the mind conjures in response. Sometimes, the best approach to take with these propositions is simply to experience them and give up on attempting to reach a rational reply. This attitude can be encapsulated in the concept of *Mu*.

Mu's meaning, at least as popularized by Robert M. Pirsig in *Zen and the Art of Motorcycle Maintenance*, is "no class; not one, not zero, not yes, not no," or, in short, "Unask the question." In other words, the inquiry does not fall into the category of questions with a concrete answer. Rather, it is intended as a tool to exercise the mind with the ultimate goal of completely bypassing thought and discovering one's true nature.

Benefits

- Working on *kōans* is a powerful path to expanding your awareness.

- *Mu* allows you to think the unthinkable and encapsulate in a word that which is inexpressible.

Challenges

- For some people, the fact that *kōans* have no correct answer can be quite frustrating.
- One can misuse *Mu* as a shortcut or as a way to avoid working with an impossible question and thus miss its fruits.

Application

There are various ways of working with *kōans*. Traditionally, Zen teachers assigned a specific *kōan* to each student with instructions to meditate on it or "walk with it" throughout the day. Students were not expected to achieve a particular correct answer but rather were judged on their overall approach. After weeks, months, or even years, the student presented a reply to their teacher, who guided them in turn using approval, disapproval, or terse further instructions. Thus, the student proceeded through a series of *kōans* with the intent of reshaping their mind and triggering a spiritual awakening.

These days, the traditional Zen method might not be suitable for everyone, especially Westerners. It's not easy to dedicate huge parts of one's life to practice. As Westerners, we are more used to bite-sized meditation, making our spiritual search one of a number of important activities in our lives, as opposed to dedicating every moment to it. If you're seeking to explore this path with a more limited commitment, you might want to practice by reading a list of *kōans* or a practice book or by listening to specific guided meditations that delve into *kōan* practice.

You may also wish to explore couples exercises, such as "Who is it?" To do this, sit facing one another. One partner looks into the other's eyes and asks, "Who are you?" The other answers with whatever comes to mind. The first partner then repeats the question, whereupon the second voices another answer, and so on. The purpose of this exercise is not to cling to these answers but rather to see them as endless false attempts to answer an unanswerable question. Behind the false answers lies valuable nonverbal insight into the truth behind the words.

Further Reading

1. "Koan," Wikipedia, https://en.wikipedia.org/wiki/Koan.
2. "Mu (negative)," Wikipedia, https://en.wikipedia.org/wiki/Mu_(negative).
3. Robert M. Pirsig, *Zen and the Art of Motorcycle Maintenance* (Mariner Books Classics, 2006).

Tool 6.5:
Find Your Moral Compass

Accept reality but simultaneously develop
a clear sense of direction.

Motivation

In certain spiritual circles, it's commonplace to subscribe to the idea that there's no good or evil, no one should be judged, and it's impossible to do wrong. While this can be a very freeing perspective, it can also lead to a lack of responsibility. If life is perfect, why should we do anything? If there are no mistakes, why fix a leaking roof? If everything is good, why earn the money to put food on the table? Why not steal whatever we need?

The answer might lie in a famous Buddhist quote, which says, "There is no right and no wrong, but right is right and wrong is wrong." This is perhaps a more comprehensive worldview, one that recognizes the need for a moral compass to guide our behavior and the potential to become better versions of ourselves.

An internal sense of values provides clarity and meaning in your life. A strong moral framework gives you a foundation you can refer to whenever you need to make a decision. The consequences of your behavior may not always unfold as you would wish, but that's okay. Whatever the outcome, knowing that you've acted in accordance with your moral compass can bring you a sense of peace.

Benefits

- A strong moral compass guides you to make wholesome choices that not only benefit you but also make the world a better place for everyone to live in.

- Referring to a deeper system of values can help you resist short-term temptations and stay aligned with your moral code.

Challenges

- There is no single right way for everyone to behave, so identifying and following your own moral compass will likely require recurring introspection.
- At times, it can be tough to remember big-picture considerations, and the easy route can appear very alluring.

Application

We do not exist in a vacuum; everything we do touches someone else, and the ripples of our choices create long-lasting consequences (see Tool 3.6 : Talk about Therapy in *Therapy*). It's important that we work on learning to accept and live happily in the present, but equally, we should understand that the choices we make will affect others, and in turn, the consequences will loop back to us. Therefore, it's important that we determine a set of principles that fulfill these conditions:

- They bring you happiness in the present.
- They improve the well-being of future incarnations of yourself (you in a day, a week, a year, etc.).
- They increase the happiness of your family, friends, humanity, and eventually the entire universe.

Crafting these principles can be challenging, and, ultimately, the journey may never end. Some are simple—as children, most of us learned to be kind, not to steal, not to intentionally hurt other people, and so forth—whereas others are more complex. When, for example, is it appropriate to tell someone a hard truth they may not want to hear?

The development of an ethical framework, however, is one of the most satisfying endeavors we can embark upon. It acts like an internal anchor, ensuring that we behave in accordance with our true values.

There are several ways to develop a moral compass. You can read and ponder the works of ethical philosophers or listen to the values espoused by society or religion. You can take the time to meditate on or journal about challenging circumstances in your own life and determine the best path forward. Alternatively, you can rely on your intuition to tell you how to behave. Whatever approach—or combination of approaches—you choose, ultimately, your moral compass must feel like your own so you can rely on it to anchor your decisions.

Further Reading

1. Jordan Peterson, *12 Rules for Life: An Antidote for Chaos* (Random House, 2018).

2. Religious texts (e.g., the Bible's Ten Commandments, Buddhism's Five Precepts, etc.).

3. Sam Harris, *The Moral Landscape: How Science Can Determine Human Values* (Free Press, 2011).

Tool 6.6:
Anattā (Non-Self)

The Buddhist concept that the experience of a distinct self is an illusion.

Motivation

According to Buddhism, the source of suffering is the illusion of self—that is, the ubiquitous belief that there exists a unique, separate, and unchanging part inside us that constitutes a consistent "Me" and to which things happen. This makes everything, including suffering, *personal*—we find ourselves thinking, "I am suffering," which in turn increases our suffering. Buddhists believe this is a trick our mind plays on us and that when we observe reality experimentally, we will discover that this "Me" is illusory. If you want to reduce or eliminate your suffering or just to know yourself in the deepest sense, this belief is worth exploring.

Benefits

- Experiencing the self as merely an illusion can allow us to weather pain more easily without compounding it by heaping needless suffering on top.

- The idea that others also lack a definitive self can reduce the need to blame and judge them, defusing situations that might otherwise lead to conflict.

- There is an intrinsic value in seeing things as they truly are.

Challenges

- The concept that there is no self seems to go against our usual experience, making it hard to understand, trust, and apply.

- The road to encountering the non-self is not always clear, and instructions on attaining this state can seem nonsensical before one experiences it.
- Can be misapplied, leading to nihilism and a loss of meaning.

Application

Proponents of anattā suggest many different routes to the realization of selflessness, ranging from meditation (see Tool 6.1: Meditation), listening to spiritual teachers, psychedelic drugs, experiments such as the Headless Way,[9] and many more. The key thing to understand here is that you don't currently have a self that you are seeking to lose. Rather, there already *is* no self—indeed, there never has been—and the key to recognizing this is a *change of perspective* revealing that you are not the illusory self you may appear to be. However, this is not something you are asked to believe in as an act of faith but rather something you should test out on your own.

Therefore, the realization of anattā always takes place in the present moment. But, for most of us, it slips away repeatedly. We forget that we are not ourselves, and the illusion raises its head all over again. The only way to address this is to be mindful in every moment in order to repeatedly wake up to this reality. Indeed, the very goal of reaching a state of permanent freedom from this illusion, otherwise known as enlightenment, is a story that distracts us from being free in the here and now (see Tool 6.7: Enlightenment Is Always Now).

Also, be aware that the realization of anattā is not binary. It's entirely possible to loosen our identification with our sense of self gradually or partially, which can lessen the experience of suffering. Any move in this direction can help, even if we cannot wholly accept that we are without a self.

---

[9] The Headless Way: https://headless.org/.

Further Reading

1. A related concept, dependent origination: "Pratītyasamutpāda," Wikipedia, https://en.wikipedia.org/wiki/Prat%C4%ABtya samutp%C4%81da.

2. "Emptiness, or Śūnyatā," Lion's Roar, https://lionsroar.com/buddhism/emptiness-sunyata/.

3. Satyendra Kumar Pandey, "Anattā to Śūnyatā," *International Journal of Multidisciplinary Trends* 4 no. 1(2022): 17-20, https://multisubjectjournal.com/article/112/4-1-11-448.pdf.

4. "Interdependence and Non-Self (Anattā)," Fiveable, last updated July 22, 2024, https://library.fiveable.me/introduction-buddhism/unit-6/interdependence-non-self-anattā/study-guide/WQcD3xI9EH5v6r2p.

Tool 6.7:
Enlightenment Is Always Now

Enlightenment isn't a goal to pursue; it exists in the present.

Motivation

People often embark on their spiritual path after seeking various material goals, such as money or power. After a while, they realize these goals are empty and don't lead to happiness, and they begin to seek spiritual goals, especially perpetual enlightenment. They often think that enlightenment is a goal to pursue, and once they reach it, they will be permanently enlightened from that point onward. This point of view usually only adds to their suffering by generating new goals, along with more dissatisfaction with the way things are and with what's missing from the present moment.

Some people have peak experiences, in which they feel complete bliss and total satisfaction within the present moment, which can feel like heaven, nirvana, or enlightenment. Then, after a few hours, days, or weeks, the realities of life come back to them, and they lose this state of mind. When this happens, they usually crave a permanent return to that blissful mindset, which only increases their suffering.

If you can learn to accept that enlightenment is neither a permanent state to attain nor a goal to pursue, this realization can diminish your suffering and help you stay present in the current world.

Benefits

- Acknowledging that perpetual enlightenment is a story can help you be more present and aware.
- Not being tied to a rigid goal frees us up to explore life and spirituality with greater flexibility and openness.

Challenges

- People who've had peak spiritual experiences tend to develop a craving for perpetual enlightenment.

- Gurus and historical figures like Jesus and Buddha may inspire people to believe that enlightenment is a goal to be achieved, and this belief (true or false) can be an obstacle to being in the here and now.

Application

There is a paradox inherent in pursuing the idea that enlightenment isn't a goal. Nonetheless, there are different approaches to reaching this realization.

For some, meditation (see Tools 6.1: Meditation and 6.8: Beware of Spiritual Ego) can do the trick. Meditation helps you see through your thoughts and stories, bring you to the present, and experience the realization that there is no "you" inside your mind that needs to be enlightened. For others, psychedelic experiences can offer this insight. Still, others can reach that state simply by taking a walk in nature or through repeated sessions with a teacher or meditation group (called a sangha).

A better way to view enlightenment might be as a trait we always possess but of which we aren't always aware. There is no one path to access enlightenment. Once you do, sooner or later you are likely to forget this realization and return to your usual goal-oriented mind, with enlightenment as one of your goals. However, once you have had the experience that all goals in life are made up, it will be easier for you to remember and re-experience this in the future.

Further Reading

1. Jack Kornfield, *After the Ecstasy, the Laundry* (Bantam, 2001).
2. Sam Harris, *Waking Up: A Guide to Spirituality Without Religion* (Simon & Schuster, 2015).
3. Waking Up app: https://wakingup.com/.

Tool 6.8:
Beware of Spiritual Ego

Resist the urge to treat spirituality as a competition.

Motivation

When we embark on a path of spiritual inquiry, our default attitude is to approach this process with the same goal-oriented mindset we are used to applying in other areas of our lives. This can twist spirituality into something we excel at, potentially obscuring the reasons why we began this journey in the first place.

For example, we may set the goal of reaching a state of enlightenment or compare ourselves with friends and seek to be more spiritual than them—whatever that means—perhaps as an attempt to win the approval of a respected teacher or parent.

This type of competitive spirituality can prevent us from realizing the principles of our chosen path, as, ironically, can its opposite—abandoning or attempting to kill the ego. The solution lies somewhere in the middle—true enlightenment is found in the acceptance of all things, including the ego.

Benefits

- Focusing on yourself is more effective than making comparisons with others.
- Breaking the spell cast by the goal-oriented mind can propel us into deeper self-realization.
- Recognizing the ego-driven nature of too much spiritual searching releases us from the need to be perfect, which can free up a lot of energy and reduce stress.

Challenges

- Modern society tends to engage our goal-oriented mind, so letting go of this mindset can feel very unfamiliar.
- This concept can easily be misinterpreted to suggest that there's no point in making any spiritual effort or trying to do anything at all.

Application

When we take an interest in spirituality, the role of the ego becomes particularly thorny. Some of us pursue spiritual objectives with an ego-driven zeal, betraying an underlying desire to somehow become the best or the most spiritual.

At the other end of the scale, we may be tempted to try to remove ego from our lives entirely, which is a form of spiritual bypassing. When this takes hold, we may seek to prove how little ego we have, an impulse that ironically emerges from the ego. Or, we may lose the drive that pushes us toward accomplishments, concluding that this drive is an expression of the ego and, therefore, invalid.

At the heart of this perspective is a paradox. The ego drives us to act in the world, earn money, achieve goals, improve, and become something. If we subscribe to the viewpoint that we should not do any of these things in order to reach a higher level of spiritual attainment, then we are denying a part of our existence. It's likely that the ego will emerge in other ways, such as via a competition to be more spiritual than others.

Enlightened masters teach us that a true spiritual path lies somewhere in the middle—accepting the wiles of the ego, yet not holding onto them too tightly. A famous quote attributed to the Zen monk Shunryu Suzuki Roshi asserts that "enlightenment is an accident, but spiritual practice makes us accident-prone." In other words, we cannot become enlightened through mere striving, but certain practices increase the chances of seeing through the illusions of this world and perceiving immortal truths.

The key to breaking through the paradox of spiritual ego is acceptance. Spiritual practices such as meditation and contemplation can be an important way to cultivate acceptance, as long as they are focused not on being better than others but on being okay with where we are. An entirely ego-driven existence, for example, trying to find meaning and purpose in life by chasing after money, material goods, or sexual partners, is unlikely to bring true fulfillment. On the other hand, suppressing the desire for a successful career and the attainment of challenging goals can leave us feeling equally empty. The middle path—accepting our human needs and desires—is the route to peace and balance.

Further Reading

1. "ARJ Barker, Sickest Buddhist": https://www.youtube.com/watch?v=Pbzs_5gD2DM.

2. "Homer Simpson - Trying Is The First Step Towards Failure. Wise Advice on Trying Something": https://www.youtube.com/watch?v=dhrEzA3SEBU.

3. Eva Beronius, "What Is a Spiritual Ego?" Self Mastery and Beyond, March 24, 2021, https://selfmasteryandbeyond.com/blog/what-is-a-spiritual-ego/.

Tool 6.9:
Watch Out for Cults/False Gurus

Some spiritual leaders and groups can be dangerous.

Motivation

The outcomes of most things you may wish to learn can be easily measured. If you want to play better golf, you engage a golf instructor. You will soon know whether he's good at his job because you will see measurable improvements in your game and your scores.

Spirituality, on the other hand, is almost impossible to measure. There's no externally verifiable scale of spiritual growth, so both assessing your own progress and discerning the spiritual development of others is subjective. This makes it much harder to discern whether someone is a qualified spiritual teacher. Some people who call themselves spiritual leaders are brimming with charm and charisma and hold out tempting promises of enlightenment and inner peace. They may or may not live up to these claims, and their legitimacy can be hard to evaluate. Furthermore, some might actually be dangerous! Therefore, you should listen to your own inner wisdom and decide for yourself.

Benefits

- Exercising your own judgment and critical thinking is a valuable skill to develop in any context.
- A little well-placed skepticism can protect you from potentially dangerous religious groups.
- If you avoid wasting energy on false paths, you'll be free to explore and find paths that do work for you.

Challenges

- If you are already enmeshed in a cult, it can be hard to get out. Sometimes, you don't realize you are part of a dangerous organization until you are fully entrenched.

- It's possible to become *too* suspicious and miss out on spiritually enriching life experiences.

Application

If you're questioning whether you should belong to a group or follow a particular leader, you can compare the behaviors of the leaders and the group's expectations with characteristics of known cults or false gurus. In particular, there are three warning signs to watch out for:

1. **All power in an organization stems from the leader.**

   When a spiritual leader claims ultimate authority in spiritual matters, this is often a dangerous red flag. They may reinforce this attitude by creating a mythologized origin story about how they reached such a high spiritual plane, by dismissing the insights of others, or by maintaining a ritualized separation between themselves and other members of the group. This is sometimes evidenced by awarding special privileges, such as gifts and acts of service, to leaders, often in ways that cross sexual or other boundaries.

2. **The creation of in- and out-groups.**

   This can take several forms. For example, the world within a cult may be upheld as beautiful, pure, and special, juxtaposed against the corrupted or fallen world outside. Another possibility is the use of specialized jargon, understood only within the context of a cult, that conveys a sense of separation. The leader may also distinguish themselves from other spiritual lineages to place themselves beyond comparison and, therefore, criticism. One key sign of this tendency is when a group discourages, limits, or even prohibits contact with those they deem outsiders, including friends and family.

3. Weaponizing peak experience and healing.

Cultic spiritual groups may impose tightly controlled conditions on sex, prayer, breathwork, dance, and drugs. Only those deemed worthy are allowed to access these techniques, creating a way to reward and punish followers. This approach may be reinforced by emphasizing the value of feeling over thinking—for example, encouraging members to "follow their heart" or "trust their gut." This could also mean pressuring people to make consequential social, financial, or emotional commitments while they are in euphoric states and feel deeply bonded to other members of the group.

A powerful antidote to falling in with such groups or coming under the spell of charismatic yet dangerous individuals is listening to your own voice, checking in with what's right for you, and knowing what falls outside of your boundaries. In addition to the signs listed above, you should take the time and space you need to really listen to yourself rather than to other people's suggestions about what's supposedly good for you. To that end, you can try Tool 6.1: Meditation or Tool 3.4: Talk to Your Inner Selves.

Further Reading

The Ethical Cult Checklist: https://uploads-ssl.webflow.com/5e74e 8349194e2f76b9ffcd1/5e754938d25345a72291f0a3_Ethical%20 Cult%20Checklist.pdf.

Tool 6.10:
Conversations with God

Access a source of infinite wisdom and love.

Motivation

In Neale Donald Walsch's book *Conversations with God: An Uncommon Dialogue*, the author details his own discussion with God. The book opens with Walsch writing down his most important questions about life without expecting any answers. To his surprise, he finds himself responding to his own questions from a different perspective, which he interprets as guidance from a higher power.

This tool can work for you whether you consider yourself a believer, an atheist, or agnostic. The concept of God—or a sense of the divine as the entirety of everything that has been, is, and will one day be—can be an important psychological and spiritual touchstone. You may even consider these dialogues a specific use-case of Tool 3.4: Talk to Your Inner Selves. Connecting with your representation of God verbally can be a powerful way to access meaning and wisdom when encountering personal obstacles or tackling big questions, such as "Why am I here?" or "What is this life about?"

Benefits

- Conversing with whatever God means to you can unlock a strong sense of meaning and purpose.
- This process can awaken feelings of being loved and accepted unconditionally.
- This dialogue may provoke unexpected inspiration and surprising answers.

Challenges

- If your skepticism dominates the process, you may find it hard to open up.

- You may feel like you're faking it and that your answers aren't truly coming from the infinite.

Application

To begin, settle yourself in a quiet place and prepare yourself for a conversation. How you do this is up to you. Neale Donald Walsch wrote out his questions, then allowed God to write the answers through him. You could also utilize other means such as meditation, floating in a pool, talking to yourself out loud, or doing anything that doesn't require your single-minded focus. Regardless of method, it's important that you begin with the intention of engaging with a higher power. The key is to open yourself up, release any resistance you may be feeling, and express what's alive in you . . . then listen for an authentic response.

Open yourself up and invite replies as though you are really conversing with a higher power. Let go of any doubts you have about whether God exists and simply surrender to the experience. If you get frustrated with the process or with the answers you receive, that's okay—express your frustration! Whatever you're feeling, be as honest as you can and share it openly.

You might ask questions such as, "What should I do with my life?" or "Should I take job A or job B?" and not necessarily like the answers you get. It's important to understand that God—whether a real being or your psychological conception of the divine—isn't here to solve your problems and live your life for you. She's here to be with you and to live and express through you. [10]

---

[10] God probably doesn't have a gender, but language demands the use of one. Referring to God as "She" seemed at least as appropriate as using "He."

According to Neale Donald Walsch, God is the infinite totality of everything and chose to take limited form and split into finite components in order to experience separateness. Being omnipotent makes it impossible to feel the joys and pains that limited beings experience, which is why you, as a distinct expression of the divine, matter.

Further Reading

Neale Donald Walsch, *Conversations with God: An Uncommon Dialogue* (Hodder & Stoughton, 1997).

CONCLUSION

Thank you for reading this far. Hopefully, you've discovered a few tools that are already serving you on your life's journey. We all travel many paths over the years, and we therefore need a variety of tools at the ready to serve us in different times and situations. We cannot apply everything in this book to our lives all the time—that would be overwhelming and counterproductive.

Keep in mind that not all tools will work for everyone at all times. You may find one that is perfect for you right now but that will not work at a later date, even in a similar situation. The opposite is also true—a technique that doesn't sit well with you now could be perfect in the future. In some cases, you may know immediately that a tool is right for you, while others may require a period of adjustment or practice before they feel natural and useful. Every step forward is a success, and you can reap partial benefits from tools even without applying them to their full extent.

Here's another thing to remember as you go forward: Per the Meta tool we discussed at the beginning of the book, none of us will ever reach a point where we cannot possibly improve a single thing in our lives. To be alive is to be in a perpetual state of evolution, inevitably revisiting familiar situations. When we have a carefully tailored system, we boost our odds of success. And, of course, if we can constantly tweak our approach to match our existing circumstances, then our odds of success improve even more.

What Next?

I've invested many hours curating and describing the tools in this book. In each case, I have done my best to capture the essence of each tool. Inevitably, however, I'm not perfect, and I may have introduced errors or simply missed elements of these tools. Like writing a book, life is an iterative process—if you notice any mistakes, wish to suggest additions or edits, or have anything else to share, your feedback is very welcome. You can reach me directly via https://ripper234.com/.

Looking forward, my goal is to collaborate with others and expand this collection to cover many more tools. I did start this process, but the tools contained within these pages don't belong to me. They are a resource for everyone and are available freely at https://whateverworks. me/. If you have ideas for new tools or even entirely new chapters, you're invited to contribute.

The contents of this book form the basis of a small community of people committed to self-development. If you're interested in discussing any aspect of the tools, such as which ones work best for you or how to apply them, you're invited to join the Whatever Works community at the "Community" section on the above website.

This project has been a labor of love over the course of several years, and I hope the publication of this book will be just the start of a larger journey. I'd like to think that if we all use the tools here to become just a little bit better every day, we can each contribute to making the world a little better and together end up making a big difference. May you always have the right tools for the challenges that lay in your path.

ACKNOWLEDGMENTS

First of all, thanks to you, the reader, for joining this journey and giving these tools your trust, time, and attention. I hope they've repaid you amply.

Thanks, too, to the originators of the tools you find in this book. A few came from me, but most were created by others, recently or long ago. I couldn't have written this book without your work.

Writing this book has been a long process, and many people have contributed along the way. Looking back, I wish I'd kept a more exhaustive list of who helped where. This is my best recollection—in many cases, people who assisted significantly with one tool also had a hand in others.

Yoad Rowner, thanks for your invaluable contributions to Getting Things Done and other Productivity tools.

Eran Teicher, thanks for your detailed feedback on Nonviolent Communication and your work on numerous other tools, especially in the Therapy chapter.

Andreas Hultgren, Renee Tawil, Arthur Havlicek, Ian Hartnell, David Rozenthal, Talia Michaeli, Sharon Shineberg, and Leon Hazan (King Bear), thanks for reading and sharing your feedback and for your support. If you contributed to the book and I've forgotten to mention you here, my apologies. Your efforts are appreciated!

A big thank you goes to the team who helped create this book. Thanks to the two scribes I worked with via Scribe Media—Lisa Shiroff and Rob Wolf Petersen. We've spent many, many hours together connecting, exploring, nitpicking over words, and trying to find clear ways to convert ideas and meaning into text. It's been a true pleasure. Also, thanks to Helene Webb and the rest of the team at Ballast Books for continuing the publishing work and community building and helping me revive this project after it suffered a major injury. All of you have been super professional.

Liat Zioni Morad, thanks for editing some of these tools, accompanying this project for years, handling communications, setting up the website and wiki, and many other tasks, both large and small. I appreciate you sharing this path with me.

Finally, a special thank you goes to Anat Rapoport for co-creating and editing Mega Threads and other tools and also for being there for me and supporting me through these long years and multiple challenges. An author's journey is a lonely and difficult one, but you have made it more bearable.

ABOUT THE AUTHOR

Ron Gross is dedicated to the convergence of technology, self-improvement, and community-driven innovation. With an MSc in computer science from the Technion, Ron has extensive experience in both tech and leadership, primarily in small startups, but also in corporate life at Google.

An early adopter of Bitcoin and a cryptocurrency advocate since 2011, Ron has long been passionate about decentralization, transparency, and open-source technologies. He co-founded the Israeli Bitcoin Association and served as the executive director of the Mastercoin Foundation, leading the first-ever ICO.

Today, Ron focuses on leading his startup Fredo.ai, a WhatsApp productivity bot, while exploring practical tools for optimizing life, enhancing productivity, and nurturing meaningful relationships. Connect with Ron at https://ripper234.com/.